Warfare

ROBERT HARRISON

University of Wisconsin
Milwaukee

Burgess Publishing Company • Minneapolis, Minnesota

A SERIES ON
BASIC CONCEPTS IN ANTHROPOLOGY
Under the Editorship of
A. J. Kelso, University of Colorado
Aram Yengoyan, University of Michigan

Contents

Introduction

Civil Strife and Invasion, the two of the Four Horsemen of the Apocalypse which represent warfare, have led a checkered career throughout the course of history, in the minds of men. Toward the other members of this famed cavalry, Pestilence (plague) and Famine, mankind has perhaps recorded a more consistent attitude. While famine and pestilence have almost always been regarded as abominations, warfare has, at times, been regarded as the means by which the millenium would be achieved and the agent through which a better social order might be produced. Few persons have regarded famine and disease in the same light.

Those who gained renown in relation to disease, such as Walter Reed, Louis Pasteur, the Curies, Goethals, Salk and Sabine, to name but a few, are those who gained their fame in the fight against disease. To fight, however heroically, against warfare is hardly likely to gain one the esteem of one's fellow citizens. The number of conscientious objectors who have become national heroes is infinitesimally small. Most Americans are aware, via one form of media or another, of the bravery and daring of such men as Geronimo, Cochise, and Sitting Bull. Few, however, know of the courage and the trials and tribulations of Black Kettle, a very peaceful Arapaho/Cheyenne leader (Brown 1972: 77-169). The heroes of warfare are those who have gained renown in battle, not against it. And, it is more usually the character and attributes of the warrior—bravery in the face of danger, stoicism in the face of pain, and aggressiveness—that we would wish upon our children. At present, the X-rated films are not war films.

Our histories are predominantly histories of warfare and our heroes predominantly warriors. Even when our heroes are from other professions, as is the case with the above-named bacteriologists, it is in terms of the attributes of the warrior that we attempt to characterize their efforts and to understand them. Murphy's critique of history as a discipline (1971: 105), has some meaning for anthropology as well:

The criteria of relevance and significance are commonly those that present themselves to us through the medium of our own society, in part because we

1

are products of that society . . . . Wars, kings, and revolutions are important: these are Big Facts. Work, family, and habitation are less unique to their times and less exciting to our imaginations: these are Little Facts.

While anthropology is undoubtedly a science of Little Facts, it is the Little Facts of Big Fact societies which we find most interesting. It could hardly be otherwise, as anthropologists are as much a product of their societies as are historians.

Some small indication of the degree to which warfare and battle are important in our society may be gained by examining the way in which we characterize other events in terms of combat. Scanning the current issue of the Books In Print catalogue (1971) one finds the following interesting usages in book titles, to list but a few: Battle Against Bacteria; Battle Against Heart Disease; Battle Against Poverty; Battle for Stock Market Profits; Battle for the Free Mind; Battle to Breathe; War Against Poetry; War of the Theatres; War on Time; War on Want. It would appear that, however much we may abhor war, the tendency to characterize our activities and social movements in terms of combat is fairly pronounced. It is little wonder, therefore, that McNeil (1965) utilizes the introduction in his reader, *The Nature of Human Conflict*, to raise the question of our objectivity, rather than using the introduction in its more usual role. It would appear that McNeil, as others, has some doubts about our capacity to be at peace with the subject of warfare.

Warfare, as it will be considered here, is viewed simply as an attack, or acts of aggression, by members of one social group upon members of another portion of the same group (civil strife) or upon members of a different social group. Such attacks, or acts of aggression, should broadly be construed as having at least some tacit support among the members of the group initiating and/or perpetuating the hostilities. It is not required that the members of the group being attacked in any way accept or approve of the hostilities being visited upon them.

While such definition in no way excludes spouse beating and the forms of feuding practiced in the past by the fabled Hatfields and McCoys, this author would like to appeal to the reader for their exclusion on two grounds. Firstly, both are types of familial violence which generally occur within the framework of a largely disapproving social structure—even where wife beating is permitted by law this does not make it socially acceptable to the immediate social group, the neighborhood, or community; moreover, such acts of violence are not acts of warfare as we generally have come to know it, however undefined that knowledge may be. Secondly, the author appeals to the philosophical doctrine of "sweet reasonableness" in the belief that, in terms of furthering discussion, no purpose will be served by demanding at this point an overprecise and overly exclusive definition of the types of acts which should or should not be considered "warfare."

Explanations of warfare take as their initial premise either of two possible postulates. The first (and perhaps the most philosophically pessimistic) is that warfare is inherent among men. Obviously the second postulate is that it is not inherent. Or, to state the second position more positively, war is a social phenomenon. While the causes of war must be empirically verified in each case, such causes when adduced are likely to give evidence of some form of socioeconomic, socioecologic, or sociocultural disequilibrated situation. Such disequilibrated situations might be unbalanced land/man ratios (Vayda 1971), intertribal man/woman ratios (Divale 1970), man/animal ratios (Sweet 1965), vying for strategic location in the passage of essential goods (Hunt 1940), too great an imbalance within or between systems of stratification with regard to access to the strategic resources of an area or industry, or unbalanced resource use by peoples at different levels of technology. Other causal explanations are psychological dependence (Murphy 1957), schismo-genesis (Bateson 1967), and just a general cultural acceptability of warfare as an alternative to internal states of social or psychological tension. While this by no means exhausts the possible list, it does highlight the more general types of situations cited as causes of war which are socially initiated.

For those who take the position that warfare is inherent, such immediate causes as listed above would be abstracted to a higher level of explanation, and discussion of cause would center around such concepts as "intraspecific aggression and arousal mechanisms," "territoriality," "frustration due to intragroup complexities," etc. Those who view warfare as inherent are divided into at least two camps. The first are those who see warfare as a product of a genetically transmitted mode of aggression acquired at some point in the phylogenetic history of the species. Warfare is therefore biologically induced behavior.

Others who see warfare as inherent see it not as a genetically transmitted mechanism but as a product of social life. That is, warfare is a synergistic result of man living in social groups. Warfare is social, not genetically transmitted behavior; ergo it is one of the unfortunate products of group behavior.

In terms of this latter position there are two further distinctions possible. The first is that held among those social scientists who view social life as a process somewhat akin to either the Hegelian dialectic (ideas, ideation, and norms are the motive and guiding force generating and channelizing social behavior) or the Marxian dialectic (ideas and conscience are the products of social being). A dialectical process is one whereby any new form, be it ideational or real behavior, is the product of the clash between two forces, labelled in Hegelian terms as the "thesis and antithesis," whose very interaction produces the new form of dialectic, perhaps the ultimate one, along a continuum of possible conflicts. A more modern theoretical usage of the model of the dialectical process is to be found in the works of Ralf Dahrendorf, whose theory of conflict will be discussed in a later portion of this paper. It is sufficient to say here that Dahrendorf's dialectical process is thoroughly sociological. Unlike Marx, who saw conflict arising out of the members of a social group who have differential relations to the modes of production, Dahrendorf sees conflict arising between the members of a society who share differential relationships to the structure of authority.

Another distinction is the Freudian one which sees individual needs and the social order as antithetical. The relation between these needs and the society is also viewed as a dialectical process but here, however, the level of explanation is psychological rather than sociological. As group demands are backed by more power and force than the individual can usually muster, and, as the group offers the person the greatest potential for survival and ultimate fulfillment, the individual surresses or sublimates his aggressive drives to perpetuate his place in the group and to further group life itself. Conflict and ultimately warfare erupt, since these processes which relate man to his society must necessarily be incomplete. As Murphy (1971: 71) interprets Freud's view of this process of internalization:

In any event, internalization was always a sloppy, incomplete, and tension-fraught process to Freud, for it is in eternal contradiction to the asocial component of man's nature.

In any society it is possible that the demands of today are not likely to be the demands of tomorrow. Thus the trajectories of change between man and society, man and man, society and society are often likely to be slightly out of register. What we suppress today is in demand tomorrow; what we now disparage and disallow we may have most recently enjoyed. Warfare here may be the result of cumulative frustrations which a society places upon its members. The perpetuation of warfare may be a means of expressing, in socially acceptable form—and often an heroic one—behavior which in other circumstances would be considered socially unacceptable.

Biological
Explanations
of Warfare

OUR ANIMAL INHERITANCE

In recent times, the major advocates who seek explanations of man's social behavior in his animal past have been Konrad Lorenz (1970), Robert Ardrey (1971), and Desmond Morris (1969). These are the supporters of this position whose works have been most widely disseminated and most popularly received. They see much of our social behavior, and hence many of our problems, as being related to the conditions laid down by and rooted in our basic animal nature. Often the problems we face are not just the result of our animal inheritance but the result of our failure to live in accordance with our animal natures. Each of these men have researched, in their own ways, various aspects of that animal inheritance. Lorenz, whose work is of immediate interest to us, reviews the phylogenetic history of aggression; Ardrey investigated mainly problems of territoriality; Morris, being more catholic in his tastes, has ranged over broad areas of human and animal behavior.

These authors attempt to demonstrate the proposition that many of the particular biological features with which we are endowed, such as enlarged cranial capacities, opposable thumbs, stereoscopic vision, etc., as well as our propensities in and for social life were acquired as solutions to problems faced in our evolutionary march through the class *Mammalia* and more particularly through the order *Primatata*. As Morris (1969: 21) states:

All we had to go on, as animals, was a set of biological characteristics evolved during our long hunting apprenticeship. The answer must lie in the nature of these characteristics and the way we have been able to exploit and manipulate them. . . .

Bearing in mind our monkey ancestry, the social organization of surviving monkey species can provide us with some revealing clues.

Often these clues are to be found in observed similarities between animals and man, and often this involves a direct translation and the implicit

5

assumption of cognate status for the behavior so observed as the following passages from Morris's (1969: 42-43) work reveal:

You must clearly display the trappings, postures and gestures of dominance.

For the baboon this means a sleek, beautifully groomed, luxuriant coat of hair; a calm, relaxed posture when not engaged in disputes. . . .

With a few superficial modifications, the same holds true for the human leader. The luxuriant coat of fur becomes the rich and elaborate costume of the ruler. . . . He assumes postures unique to his dominant role.

For Lorenz aggression in man has the status of instinct. He views it as a form of behavior which has become locked into our genetic structure. This occurred because at some point in our phylogenetic past those of our burgeoning species who were aggressive survived longer to reproduce than those who lacked this trait. Intraspecific aggression—which in its most intense form would be warfare—he hypothesizes as having come into being in the Early Stone Age in somewhat of the following manner (1970: 39):

Above all, it is more probable that the destructive intensity of the aggression drive, still a hereditary evil of mankind, is the consequence of a process of intraspecific selection which worked on our forefathers for roughly forty thousand years, that is throughout the Early Stone Age. When man had reached the stage of having weapons, clothing, and social organization, so overcoming the dangers of starving, freezing, and being eaten by wild animals, and these dangers ceased to be the essential factors influencing selection, an evil intraspecific selection must have set in. The factor influencing selection was now the wars waged between hostile neighboring tribes. These must have evolved in an extreme form of all those so-called "warrior virtues" which unfortunately many people still regard as desirable ideals.

If warfare became locked into our instinctual behavioral repertoire in this manner perhaps the "warrior virtues" are equally instinctual behavior. In that case they would hardly be unfortunate, just genetic. Lorenz's position is an extraordinarily pessimistic point of view, especially in light of his "avowal of optimism" with which he ends the book.

The relation between behavior and genetic structure cannot be dismissed lightly, however. All of the physical apparatus and physiological features and systems which we possess collectively are part of our genetic endowment. Where selective pressures operate man changes either by migrating, adapting physiologically, adapting culturally, or dying off. A case in point is that of the South American Indians of the High Andes. In a low oxygen environment where there were selective pressures for developing means of increasing the efficient use of available oxygen they developed larger lung capacities and red blood cells which are capable of carrying more oxygen than their counterparts in the lowlands.

Our behavioral repertoire is definitely limited by what is biologically possible or potential. We cannot act, emote, or cognize in ways which are presently outside our bio-physiological potential. We can learn because we have the capacity to learn. What we learn is a result of our concrete experiences in a particular sociocultural milieu. Even here Chomsky (1970) posits that such learning and our use of our available talents may be structured by the organization of brain and the cerebral cortex in particular. The grammatical and syntactic structures of language may be channelized in this way.

Such attributes apply to the species as a whole and not to any particular segment of mankind. Though there is a good deal of evidence that throughout the history of mankind some members of the species have warred, there is no evidence that all of them have. Often the very drama with which we introduce the topic can be misleading in this way, as for instance Divale's introduction to his article (1970: 173):

In the five thousand years of civilization and in the thousands of years in the history of preliterate society warfare has been a condition of human existence.

While such a statement is true we should not be misled into believing that since man has always warred, all men have warred. Fortunately Divale is not out to prove the universality of warfare, and it is further comforting to note that he does not accept the idea that warfare is part of our biological heritage.

Gorer (1968: 34) in his review of Lorenz's work lists the Arapesh of New Guinea, the Lepchas of Sikkim, and the pygmies of the Ituri rain forest of the Congo as nonwarring peoples. To this list might be added the Tiwi of Bathhurst island off Australia. A common error within anthropology is to suppose that all the members of a group known by a particular ethnic designation who have been reported as having engaged in war have actually done so.

It could well be argued that groups which have never gone to war never would. All that can be said, however, is that they may never have been confronted with situations which would trigger their innate, programmed warfaring responses. The evidence is a counter to this. The North American

Indian groups, who generally have had the reputation for being warriors, at times, under the worst threats and under conditions of actual invasion and massacre, still sued for peace rather than fight against the invading whites.

BLACK KETTLE AND SANDY CREEK

As regards not reacting under the most compelling circumstances with hostile aggression, the story of Black Kettle, a Cheyenne/Arapaho chief, and the Sandy Creek Massacre (Brown 1972: 83-93) is instructive. Early on the morning of November 28, 1864, a force of about 700 troops, under the command of Colonel Chivington of the U.S. Cavalry, attacked Black Kettle's Cheyenne camp which had settled peacefully on a portion of Sandy Creek considered under the protection of the soldiers at Fort Lyon, Colorado. As Brown (1972: 86) states: "So confident were the Indians of absolute safety, they kept no night watch except of the pony herd. . . ." Robert Bent's eyewitness report (Brown 1972: 88) recalls:

When the troops came up to them they ran out and showed their persons to let the soldiers know they were squaws and begged for mercy, but the soldiers shot them all.

The casualties to the Cheyenne camp from that day's activity were 105 Indian women and children and 28 men dead.

Still Black Kettle would not fight, and after the massacre he moved about 400 of his people still further into the area controlled by his enemies the U.S. Cavalry. Many Cheyenne did move north and warred against the troopers by making raids on white camps for retribution. Such a varied response to the same stimulus ought to convince us that warfare is hardly likely to be a genetically programmed response. Further it does not seem a fair test to push an organism close to its absolute limit in order to obtain the desired response. Somehow if warfare is to be considered a genetically controlled response it should be induced somewhat short of such extremes. This is precisely the length to which we pushed many American Indian groups. That they responded as they did is hardly surprising. Their repertoire of responses short of warfare had proved totally bankrupt in dealing with whites. Under such circumstances one hardly needs heredity to explain the reaction.

It is ironic to note that for all Black Kettle's ministrations and attempts to win peace he lost his life in an almost exact replica of the Sandy Creek killing. In the early hours of the morning of November 26, 1867 (Brown 1972: 163)—just three years less two days later—the Cavalry attacked Black Kettle's camp as it slept peacefully in the valley of the Washita River, Oklahoma. The point of this episode is that the Black Kettle phenomenon, if we may for a moment call it that, is not an isolated event. People react to stress in so many different ways that one would be justified in questioning the theory of warfare as a genetically ingrained response.

One could argue that Black Kettle's actions are hardly representative. Rather it may be that as an old and tired man his behavior is simply not characteristic of the species. It should be noted, that Black Kettle's response to threat was one that occurred time after time among other American Indian groups in their relations with the white settler's expansion westward. Whatever our interpretation of Black Kettle's behavior, it is hardly likely that we could dismiss all similar cases on the same grounds.

BRAIN-SIZE, EMOTIONS, AND SOCIAL CONTROL

Another biologically based theory of aggression is to be found in the work of Ralph Holloway, Jr. Effectively his thesis is in some ways rather close to Freud's, but it does not require warfare as genetically programmed behavior to operate. In abbreviated form his argument (1968: 46-48) is as follows:

Biological evolution, in relation to man, favored the development of a large brain (specifically the cortex) as a means of dealing with the environment and achieving a higher level of task efficiency. This same development also favored the development of more finely honed arousal patterns. To the extent that adaptation was within the sphere of social behavior "increasing inhibitive controls would have been highly beneficial" (1968: 47). This process not only increased man's intellectual capacity but also gave rise to a concomitant increase in man's ability to respond emotionally which, coupled with man's social nature, aided in the process of social adaptation.

For Holloway human evolution "has been the evolution of a paradox" (1968: 48). The evolution of the complexity of the brain, the development of social structures and symbol systems, also led to increases in the levels of frustration and aggression.

The meaning of symbols in the adaptive evolutionary sense is . . . two-fold: they aid in cognitive optimization, and also, they mediate the social controls necessary to stem what arises out of the human condition, frustration and aggression (1968: 48).

In Holloway's terms this same symbolism which enhances the emotional and sentimental bonds between kinsmen also brings into being its opposite:

aggressional tendencies against those who are not members of one's own group. "Man is," therefore, "up against himself—he is up against social structure—he is up against culture" (1968: 48).

Warfare is not instinctual, nor is it caused by increased cortical size or complexity. Rather these factors have led to increases in organizational complexity, as well as increases in our cognitive and emotive range. The very ability to feel intensely attracted to something or someone is also the self-same ability to feel intensely repelled. Holloway goes on to state that warfare cannot be explained on the level of individual psychology. Warfare is a group process and can only be accounted for in terms of group behavior. To understand warfare it must be studied in terms of (1968: 48): "power, organizations, socioeconomic conditions and symbol systems. . . ." The cognitive and emotional potentialities, which all humans share, do indicate, at the level of individual psychology, the strength and forces of feelings which can be manipulated for or against certain interests within the context of a social system. Murphy (1957: 1018-1035) in his psychosocial explanation of Mundurucu warfare, to be described later, does, interestingly enough, anticipate many of the concerns expressed by Holloway.

Psychologies of Warfare

THE DISCONTENTS OF BEING CIVIL

In many respects Holloway's position is close to that of Freud, as he acknowledges (1968: 47). There is at least one important difference. Freud brings his explanation into line with and makes it dependent upon his more general theory of the unconscious. The heart of the paradox, or the crux of the dialectic, does not lie between our increased cortical capacity and complexity and social structure, as is Holloway's contention. Rather the paradox lies between man's need for society and the personal forces of the *id*, that highly generalized, volatile energy generator of the person. It is the forces of the *id* which society must control, and conflict arises where such controls are incomplete.

Another point of difference is that for Freud the constructive use of such energy must be mediated through the processes of suppression and sublimation. Suppression is the pushing out of awareness of known socially unacceptable desires, means to ends, or goals. Sublimation is the process of substituting socially acceptable ends for unacceptable ones. The instrumentalities (means) by which social goals are accomplished must be included here as it is possible to attempt permissible goals through socially sanctioned means. Sexual intercourse between consenting adults is now acceptable within our society though certain ways of achieving this blessed state have in the past been more strongly sanctioned than others. Often too, warfare is permitted between states, but the contending parties will agree on what will and will not be allowed in the way of weapons, tactics, etc.

For Freud, as may be inferred from the above statements, aggression was a negative force. This is certainly true for Lorenz as well. Both view aggression as synonomous with hostility. Lorenz sees hostility as useful in defending the group against outsiders, in spacing group members in relation to resources, and in allocating mates to potentially surviving males. It is nonetheless hostility. In Freud's terms aggression is only useful when it has been transmuted by the psychological processes defined above.

AGGRESSION, HOSTILITY, AND FRUSTRATION

Aggression is a necessary component of our lives. It is required to hunt animals, dig roots, gather foods, plant crops, and perform the many other myriad activities which make up the daily lives of all human beings. In this respect aggression is viewed as the opposite of passivity rather than as synonymous with hostility. Nor need the exaggerated movements which accompany physical aggression necessarily be viewed as hostile behavior. Most of us have observed children playing with each other in very active, aggressive ways. Such playful activity is often not negatively violent nor hostile. To view all aggression negatively is to deny ourselves the rewards of some very pleasurable activity and to increase the level of frustration which Freud and Holloway indicate we are heir to in our civilized circumstances.

Hostility, rather than being synonymous with aggression, is a special subset within the larger class of aggressive behavior. What is necessary is the development of a classification of the various forms aggression may take, some of which may involve hostility and conflict. As such, the use of aggression toward socially necessary ends and in such acts as play need not be viewed as a transformation of essentially negative forces. Aggression often is positive, useful, and immediately rewarding to the individual in and of itself.

This does not deny that individuals may experience socially unacceptable urges which need to be transformed into acceptable ends through suppression and sublimation. The etiology of such situations is likely to be very different than for the existence of aggression of itself. Only when we regard all aggression as negative culturally do we achieve the ironic position of suppressing or sublimating socially necessary forces to achieve socially acceptable ends.

Freud sees, and it is implied in Holloway, that advances in the level of civilization are accompanied by increases in the levels of frustration and hence aggression. Since aggression must be transformed the act of transformation leads to increased frustration, and on in a never ending cycle of which one of the outcomes is warfare. Such a view reflects the often held but unstated ideal of the Rousseauean concept of the Noble Savage on the one hand and the resigned acceptance of the White Man's Burden of civilization on the other. These unstated presuppositions form a romantic bias many members of highly technical civilizations feel toward the more rural and pastoral component of their own society and toward simpler societies generally.

The routinization and bureaucratization of industrial societies have their counterparts in the unending similarity of tasks in peasant agricultural systems. And it is only a romantic notion that working with one's hands, unendingly, is more rewarding than shuffling papers. Crops which don't grow may be more frustrating and the cause of more anxiety than memoranda which aren't read. The frustration an Eskimo must feel waiting at an ice hole for a seal that never comes can hardly be less than the frustration felt waiting for a tardy bus or train and the effects on the hunter's family of that which causes the frustration are likely to be even more devastating.

The corollary to the Rousseauean position is that the effects of an individual's behavior will have more consequence in a highly elaborated technologically advanced society. This position appears equally to be an affectation. The degree of social interdependence in hunting, farming, or herding societies appears to be at least equally great. The effects of socially unacceptable behavior in a small interdependent group are likely to be as immediate and as devastating. Such behavior is more likely to threaten the continued existence of the group more directly. If someone damages an electric power station it may result in our going hungry because the freezer goes off and food spoils but, after all, food can be brought in. If in a band of hunters one hunter frightens away the game, the opportunities for locating other game may be seriously reduced and no one may be around to subsidize the band. The need, therefore, for the maintenance of group norms may be greater in small societies than in larger, urban industrial ones. Frustration and aggression may arise from different sources in urban industrial society and have different consequences for their continued existence in the society, but these feelings are equally present in nonindustrial societies. That one might go to war to "resolve life's tensions, to escape from unhappiness caused by frustration in other realms of existence. . . " (Turney-High 1971: 141) is a solution as available to tribal peoples as to urban ones. Civilization may have its discontents but there are few societies without them.

Lastly, explanations at such levels of generality—the physiological and psychological predispositions of mankind, and Turney-High's (1971: 141-144) idea of psychological dependence—are of little help in understanding the events and causal trains surrounding any immediate instance of war. Sole reliance on such explanations would obscure the immediate and concrete issues involved in an armed conflict.

SCHISMOGENESIS

An important concept relevant to understanding some instances of warfare is the process termed schismogenesis, first described by Gregory Bateson in 1936 in his psychological/anthropological study, *Naven*, of the Iatmul people of New Guinea. Schismogenesis as defined (Bateson 1967: 175) is: "a process of differentiation in the norms of individual behavior resulting from cumulative interaction between individuals." Schismogenesis leads not only to greater differentiation in norms but also mutual opposition and rivalry within the context of the interaction as well (1967: 186). While Bateson describes this interactional, relational process generally in terms of individual behavior he suggests its application for groups and for understanding some of the conflict relations within and between nations as well (1967: 175; 183-184; 186; 196). It must be emphasized that this is a process that occurs not within a person or state but between persons, between groups within a state, and between states.

Such behavior may occur in either one of two forms. The first to be described is that of complementary schismogenesis. In this situation (1967: 176):

If, for example, one of the patterns of cultural behavior, considered appropriate in individual A, is culturally labelled as an assertive pattern, while B is expected to reply to this with what is culturally regarded as submission, it is likely that this submission will encourage a further assertion, and that this assertion will demand still further submission. We have thus a potentially progressive state of affairs. . . .

In more concrete terms, the demand by white settlers, the U.S., and territorial governments for more Indian land, a demand which the Indians submitted to, became part of the stimulus by which more land would be demanded. Each successive submission by the various Indian groups would, in this relationship, lead to further demands. Finally, either all Indians would be dispossessed of their land or they would refuse to submit further and thereby change the character of the relationship.

Bateson (1967: 186) suggests that such a concept may be useful in characterizing the relationships between the social groups to a class-war within a society. Each and every submission by the proletariat to the demands of the rulers would lead progressively to further demands and further submissions until some threshold might be passed which would lead to rebellion or revolution.

The second type of schismogenetic relationship is termed a symmetrical one. In this dyadic relationship the behavior of one individual or group leads the alter to respond with similar behavior (1967: 176-177).

If, for example, we find boasting as a cultural pattern of behavior in one group, and that the other group replies to this with boasting, a competitive situation may develop in which boasting leads to more boasting, and so on.

The arms race between the present world powers might be described as a relationship of this type. Such situations need not lead inevitably to war should the parties to the conflict become aware of the drift of their behavior and attempt to rectify it. It is interesting to note in this context that the refusal to dismantle the arsenals on either side of the dispute is couched in terms of the others viewing this as a form of submission and thereby using their perceived strength to make further demands. It is apparent that symmetrical relationships might evolve into complementary ones and such a solution would likely not be wholly satisfactory to both sides.

An excellent ethnographic description of such a situation in warfare is Vayda's (1971: 1-24) description of warfare among the Maring groups of New Guinea. During an engagement the:

... opposing forces took up positions close enough to each other to be within the range of arrows. Thick wooden shields, as tall as the men and about two feet six inches wide, afforded protection in combat. With the bottoms of the shields resting on the ground, warriors darted out from behind them to shoot their arrows. Some men also emerged temporarily from cover in order to taunt their foes and display bravery by drawing enemy fire.

Such behavior would continue until either both parties decided to call a halt to the proceedings by truce or until one side was routed by the other.

The potlatch of the Northwest Coast Indians, as described by Codere (1970: 1-135), might usefully be thought of as a form of symmetrical schismogenesis, as well. In this situation the feasting, gift-giving or destroying of property by one member of a group or by one group would lead eventually to an escalated response by those being hosted. This process would continue in stepwise fashion until it was no longer possible for one set of the participants to maintain or increase the intensity of interaction.

Sociocultural
Aspects of War

PSYCHOLOGICAL DEPENDENCE AND SOCIAL
STRUCTURAL NEED: THE MUNDURUCU

An excellent example of the attempt to interweave psychological and sociological principles into an explanation of the warfare of a preindustrial society is Murphy's description of warfare among the Mundurucu, in the article previously cited. The Mundurucu, who are now located "in a region of mixed forest and savannah east of the Tapajos River in the state of Para, Brazil" (1957: 1019) warred extensively during the nineteenth century. This is the period of time for which Murphy attempts to explain the presence of warfare.

Among the Mundurucu, warfare operated to maintain social cohesion by providing an outlet for frustrations and hostile feelings generated by the social organization of the group. As Murphy (1957: 1018) states:

. . . this type of social structure actually generated the bellicose activities and attitudes that functioned to preserve it, and . . . this circular relationship allowed Mundurucu society to continue through a period during which it was subjected to severe internal and external threats.

The external threats were mostly in the form of contacts with settlers from Europe, missionaries, and Brazilian local government. The internal threats appear to be, besides the structural arrangements noted, other local groups, out-migration, and what appears to be the continual threat of the loss of territory, both from the encroachment of settlers and of other indigenous groups.

The basic structural arrangements and cultural norms which predisposed members of Mundurucu society toward warfare were more or less as follows:

1. *Residence was matrilocal, and the females of each house formed a nucleus of matrilineally related kinswomen (1020).*

2. *The male—in-marrying—members of the village were of diverse local and lineal origins (1020).*

3. *Each Mundurucu village had . . . "a men's house; the latter was the locus of male activity, for all the village men slept, ate, worked and relaxed within its confines" (1020).*

4. *Each village had a chief, whose position was bolstered by the fact that his sons were generally exempt from the matrilocal residence rule (1021).*

5. *Despite the diversity of their local and lineal origins, the men of a village and ultimately the whole tribe, were expected to maintain harmonious and cooperative relations. . . . Any open show of aggression was strictly prohibited (1920).*

6. *The necessity for suppressing overt conflict as the only alternative to serious disruptions of social relations was complemented by the necessity for male cohesion and unity in villages whose hereditary inhabitants were the women. As a result, Mundurucu ethical values enjoined absolute harmony and cooperation upon all the males of the tribe (1030).*

These arrangements and norms also facilitated the operation of warfare itself. As Murphy states: "Intercommunity cooperation in warfare was facilitated by the peculiar juxtaposition of matrilocal residence and patrilineal descent" (1957:1029). Male in-married members of one village always had links to male members of other villages. Furthermore "the recruitment of men from a number of communities aggrandized their expeditions while leaving unimpaired the economic and defensive functions of villages" (1957:1029).

Mundurucu warfare was against other tribal groups, sometimes in the pay and with the weapons of the government. While booty (most often captive women and children) sometimes was taken, it apparently was not the overriding motivation for warfare. In Murphy's terms:

1. *Given the potentially centrifugal nature of leadership, descent, and residence, warfare functioned to preserve, or at least prolong, the cohesiveness of Mundurucu society (1030).*

2. *The chief was able to maintain his leadership over his lineally eclectic group of followers through his position as war leader and his complementary role as a mediator between them and Brazilian society (1030).*

3.   *. . . warfare activated and intensified male unity and values, both of which functioned to make matrilocality viable (1031).*

4.   *. . . the only way in which hostility could be unleashed without damage to the society was against the outside world (1031).*

In respect to item 4 Mundurucu divided the world into two spheres. The first was that of the Mundurucu themselves and the second was that of the *"pariwat"* (1957:1021) who were any non-Mundurucu persons. With the exception of the whites and one neighboring tribe: "all *pariwat* were enemies and . . . a proper object of attack" (1957: 1021).

If it is possible to acknowledge with Marx, C. Wright Mills, and Dahrendorf that class-structured societies are those in which there are divided interests and conflicts which arise out of the basic structure of society itself, it is not too much to concede that there may be other structural arrangements which equally promote conflict. While Murphy does not emphasize the "interests" related to the various structural groupings which make up a Mundurucu village and the society in general, it is apparent that these interests have a good deal to do with the generation of the internal conflict for which external release must be sought.

In the first instance the women who were the stable members of the community had an "interest" in the community property, resident sites, and heritable goods different from that of the in-marrying men. This condition was largely a product of post-contact change since the prior aboriginal condition was one in which the society was organized on patrilocal and patrilineal lines (Murphy 1957:1031).

Secondly, the chief and his coterie of in-marrying sons-in-law and his in-residing sons had an "interest" in maintaining the chieftainship within the boundaries of their group apart from all other men of the community. As such they existed as a group in opposition to and ruling over the rest of the men resident in the single men's dwelling, in which all were enjoined to get along. Such a stricture must have operated not only as a source of frustration for the single men but as a means of maintaining chiefly power by actually reducing the cohesion between single men.

Within the village the men, who were of diverse origins, held interests against the women who formed the stable core of the community. In the first instance they collectively held an interest in their men's house. Secondly, given the division of labor, each man maintained an allegiance to his natal community against the women of his marital community.

Finally, all Mundurucu held an interest in their society against the interest of other tribes and against Brazilian society itself. Warfare did serve notice on nearby groups that Mundurucu were warlike and thereby maintained some level of territorial integrity. The extent to which they were willing to war in the service of the whites helped them to maintain their territory as well, as Murphy notes (1957:1031). However, as Murphy also notes ironically: "Paradoxically for a people who considered all the world as an enemy, the true cause of enmity came from within their own society" (1957:1031).

WARFARE AND CONFLICT THEORY

A more general theory which sees conflict as being inherent in the social process itself is the work of Ralf Dahrendorf, mentioned earlier. Dahrendorf developed his theory as an alternative to functional theory, the main supporters of which are Talcott Parsons in sociology and Radcliffe-Brown in anthropology. In more simple terms than the subject deserves, functional theorists take equilibrium, social consensus, and system maintenance as the ends at which the behavior of the members of a society is aimed and the ends toward which the functions of the institutions of a society are directed. Murphy's analysis of warfare, written as it was in 1957, is couched not only in functional terms but describes warfare as operating so as to reinforce social cohesion and providing for system maintenance. Cohesion and maintenance are seen as the goal states of Mundurucu society.

Within anthropology a recent representative statement of this position is that made by Goodenough in his work *Description and Comparison in Cultural Anthropology* (1970: 100).

People have to work continually to maintain agreement (low variance) regarding standards, if for no other reason because of the continual dying off of older members of the community and the continual recruitment by birth of new members who do not have any knowledge of any standards at all. Seeking to learn to deal effectively with elders, on whom they depend for the accomplishment of their purposes, the young necessarily strive to develop for themselves standards of talking and behaving that will achieve the effects they desire. And the elders want the young to develop standards that bring their performance within the range of variance they are willing to accept. By precept and by reward and punishment they work to this end.

In functional terms, even conflict, as Coser (1956) demonstrates, is seen in terms of the contributions it makes toward the stasis of the society. Under such conditions it is difficult to see how change can come about. One of the major charges levelled against functional theory is that it makes no logically adequate provisions by which to explain change within the formulations of the theory. Functional theory has, for the most part, also tended to concentrate upon the normative structure of society, such that its analyses of situations often tend to describe how things ought to be rather than how they are. Observed behavior which fails to meet this criterion is either labelled as dysfunctional (if such behavior is thought not to aid in the maintenance of social cohesion) or as deviant (behavior which is seen as departing from the proscriptions of an already isolated norm).

To the extent that functional theory is a theory of stasis rather than change, it accounts for behavior which varies from observed norms in terms of deviance and dysfunction (negative ascriptions) to the extent that proponents of this position have often been accused of providing a theoretical framework for and even a championing of the status quo. Functional theory has often been seen as a politically conservative theory and as one speaking for the interests of the wealthy and the middle class rather than for the interests of all members of society. It was to these inadequacies of functional theory that Dahrendorf addressed his arguments (Dahrendorf 1959; 1967; 1968).

If Marx could say that he stood Hegel on his head by removing the dialectical process from the realm of ideas and placing it squarely in the realm of actual behavior, so too Dahrendorf might claim to have stood Parsons on his head by making conflict rather than consensus central to his social theory. In accomplishing this feat, Dahrendorf avoids the teleology implicit in the works of the functionalists. That is, within functionalism, social acts lead toward an already known end—consensus. It is not the job of the social scientists to find out what a particular institution of a society does—that is already known. What his investigation must reveal is how it does it. For Dahrendorf conflict is not the goal a society aims to achieve. Rather it is the mechanism by which a society dynamically moves from one level of operation to another. As such it might be better to say that Dahrendorf's attempt was not to stand Parsons on his head so much as it was to lay him flat.

In an excellent critique of the sociology of conflict, Angell (1965:91-115) presents in tabular form Dahrendorf's classification of conflict. This table is reproduced on the following page.

As may be demonstrated by this material conflict occurs at all levels of the social hierarchy, in terms of the differing demands placed upon the individual to the various roles he plays. While such a display is instructive, and it may be possible to erect a similar table for the various levels of conflict for nonindustrial societies, such tables do not indicate just what it is that there is conflict about.

For Dahrendorf conflict is inherent and is related to the differential

Table 1

Social Unit	1 Equal Against Equal	2 Superordinate Against Subordinate	3 Whole Against Part
A Roles	Family role vs. Occupational role	Occupational role vs. Labor-Union role	Social personality vs. Family role
B Groups	Boys vs. Girls (in class)	Father vs. Children	Family vs. Prodigal son
C Sectors	Air Force vs. Army	Manufacturers' association vs. Labor unions	Episcopalian Church vs. "High Church" group
D Societies	Protestants vs. Catholics	Free men vs. Slaves	The State vs. Criminal gang
E Suprasocietal Relations	Soviet bloc vs. Western bloc	Soviet Union vs. Hungary	Common Market vs. France

relations to authority that the members of a society have. Drawing from the material of Mundurucu society already presented, it has been shown that the sons of the chief bear a different relation to the social order and the system of authority in the community than do the rest of the in-marrying adult males or the out-marrying younger men, still in residence. Women bear a different relation to the social order than do their husbands. Each of these categories of persons, aggregates, or social groups as the case may be, essentially maintains an interest vis-à-vis the others within the social order. For Dahrendorf, an interest is "a structurally generated orientation held by the incumbents of a defined position" (Angell 1965:104).

While the relations to authority generally tend to follow the structural order of a social system so too does the access to the strategic resources of the society. For Marx it is these resources which structure relations; for Dahrendorf it is authority. We need not here argue which came first; it is sufficient to indicate that they are coordinate. In any case it hardly appears likely that most of the interests which motivate people within a society have to do with their access or lack of access to the resources of the system.

Such conflicts, which are woven into the very fabric of the social order, could effectively be resolved only by changing the social order itself. This in Dahrendorf's terms would, of course, be substituting one set of conflicts for another. Conflicts of this type are never resolved, only regulated. Much of the normative structure of a society then has to do with the regulation of conflict which is inherent.

The term conflict itself often leads one to assume that the parties to a contention maintain discordant, tangential, and often mutually exclusive values as regards the interests over which they are contending. Angell, in his critique of the sociology of conflict, makes an interesting distinction in this regard between "like values" and "common values." Anyone may possess exactly the same values as the social group or persons with whom they are contending. However, each of the contending groups may possess such a value and attempt to exclude any other group from possessing it as well. As Angell queries, "Do the nations of today value economic productivity or autonomy for anyone but themselves" (1965:111)? When we say that members of one social group hold an interest in some aspect of a social good against other members of the society this should not be construed as indicating a necessary difference in values. The values of the contending groups may be precisely the same, and differ only in terms of who they feel should be the possessor of the social good they are competing for. Such situations are examples of "like" rather than "common" or "shared" values. Often these similarities are masked, as the parties to a dispute may couch their concerns in ideological terms which maximize the difference between themselves and their competitors.

A second caution with respect to the chart is that conflict is not necessarily continuous. That is, the structured conflict at one level of the social order, such as that between husband and wife, need not lead to conflict at the next higher order of social organization, such as between lineages or clans, etc. To the extent that this is true we cannot expect to find aspects of all a society's conflicts reflected in the child-rearing patterns within the socializing unit. In this regard with respect to stratified societies, it may well be that the conflicts of the family are reflections of the conflicts that exist with the order of stratification. Such conflicts may be structured from the top down rather than the bottom up as has been the postulate of many adherents of psychological anthropology and learning theory.

If conflict is buried in the heart of social structure and shares its unique distribution as Dahrendorf hypothesizes, conflict cannot thereby be used to explain the nature of warfare, in that they have dissimilar distributions. As mentioned earlier, warfare is not universal. If we accept Dahrendorf's position we cannot accept Murphy's contention that warfare existed among the Mundurucu because there was internal conflict within the society (there is some conflict in every society or so it would appear). Warfare, again, is a special form of conflict, not continuous with, or the cumulative result of, other forms of conflict within a social order. We must look, therefore, at the particular sets of interests which have been hypothesized as the causes of war in particular instances.

WARFARE AND FEMALE INFANTICIDE

William Divale (1970:173-192) finds primitive warfare as one link in a circular causal chain, the totality of which operates to control excess population. This causal chain has as some of its other components: female infanticide, which is an attempt, perhaps, to reduce the fertility of the immediate local group; marriage alliances, an effort to distribute women between groups and cement relations with those upon whom one can rely in warfare; and polygyny, which acts to maintain warfare by creating competition between young men for the less than available females. Polygyny provides the " . . . fuel for keeping the warfare syndrome in motion through its role as a built-in source of conflict" (1970:177). Warfare thereby operates to reduce the excess male population, bringing the man/woman ratio back into line. This chain is essential as ". . . primitive birth rates are higher than death rates and that population would increase in the absence of cultural controls" (1970:177).

The key or starting point of this self-cycling chain of events, once instituted, is the practice of female infanticide. Divale (1970:174) states:

This conclusion is reached upon examination of the age-sex ratios of 112 different groups. Of the 112 societies, 91 per cent have sex ratios in the young generation where boys outnumbered girls. The average for the 112 groups is 146 boys per 100 girls. Since we know from extensive studies of different human populations that live birth sex ratios are almost equal, it can

only be concluded that extensive female infanticide is responsible for this sex imbalance. *[emphasis mine]*

Divale acknowledges, in a note, that the sex ratios at birth tend to favor males. In most societies this varies between 102 and 108 males per 100 females. Nor is it possible to ignore the possibility of female infanticide being more widespread than appears to be reported in the literature. Indeed in a recent paper Langer (1972: 93-99) has demonstrated that infanticide was an important check on population in Europe during the period 1750 to 1850. However we cannot accept the conclusion that only female infanticide could be responsible for the imbalances cited.

Among modern nations Kuwait, Guam, Singapore, Ceylon, and Pakistan have what appear to be inordinately high ratios of 177, 141, 112, 111, and 110 respectively (Bogue 1969:168). The reasons for such disbalances in census material are "high fertility and young age composition, possible under enumeration of females in the census, comparative neglect of the health of females, and in-migration of males. . ." (1969: 168). In many societies, due to their lesser mobility, their spending of more time in aggregated conditions, etc., women are more exposed to disease vectors than are men and often receive less care. Migration will often affect sex ratios in different ways. For instance in areas settled by migrating groups, if the distance from the point of origin is great and if the journey is arduous the chances are the sex ratio will be high. On short trips the ratio may well drop below 100 (Kammeyer 1969:39). Lastly, the size of a group itself will affect, at any given point in time, the sex ratio for any given age/sex cohort. In small, isolated societies such as are to be found on many Pacific Islands the total population size may be around 200 persons, with about five or six breeding families. In such situations sex ratios are subject to sample error in that one family producing an imbalance of one sex children over another will disproportionately affect the total sex ratio.

Also, rather unfortunately, the census data from the 112 societies Divale cites is entirely unconvincing. Most of the data are drawn from censuses of the late nineteenth and early twentieth century—a period of rather extreme contact, the effects of which cannot be discounted. For instance, the range of censused years for the data presented on North American Indians is 1715 to 1931 with the bulk of material falling in the late nineteenth century. Divale recognizes some of these problems of census data thusly (1970:174):

. . . *when a colonial government took over an aboriginal area the first order of business was pacification of that area, that is, they put a stop to the warfare. Then missionaries usually moved in, and finally, a decade or so later the colonial governments would take a census of the conquered peoples.*

What Divale never deals with is the effect of this pacification on the aboriginal population itself. Among many of the American Indian groups whose figures are cited such pacification was tantamount to extermination. Attacks by the military on Indian communities and camps often resulted in a larger number of deaths for women and children [some of whom were girls] than for young men and warriors, as the Battle of Sandy Creek, recounted earlier, indicates. The type of situation represented by Sandy Creek is not an isolated incident in the settlement of North America, South America, and other now Third World areas as well. Even today the bombing and artillery barrages on villages in Vietnam, as reported, killed more women and children than suspected soldiers.

Secondly, among the Indians forced onto reservations many starved to death. This situation again was sexually selective as many of the younger men could and did leave the reservation grounds to hunt. The trails and forced marches to these areas often took their toll differentially as well. Diseases of which the aboriginal population were relatively free became rife under the more crowded, less plentiful conditions of the pacified reservations. The effects of contact with colonial/industrial nations on aboriginal populations generally has, for the most part, been so traumatic that one can hardly use the population statistics for very many purposes at all. To quote Sir George Grey [out of Sahlins 1972:8] " . . . the anthropology of hunters is largely an anachronistic study of ex-savages—an inquest into the corpse of one society . . . presided over by members of another." It does not appear that we can accept Divale's infanticide-marriage alliance-polygyny-warfare syndrome as having as universal an applicability as his data suggests might be the case.

WARFARE, POPULATION, AND RESOURCE DISTRIBUTION
The Marings of New Guinea
Vayda, who has made the largest number of recent contributions to the anthropological study of warfare (1960; 1961; 1961 with Leeds; 1967; 1968; 1971), presents another systemslike model of warfare in which population is one of the principal components. The material presented here is from his article on war and peace among the Marings of New Guinea which appeared in the journal *Oceania* in 1971.

Very generally the Marings are a group of some 7000 people living in an area of about 190 square miles in the Simbai and Jimi Valleys of the Bismarck Range located just to the northeast of Mount Hagen in the Eastern New Guinea Highlands. Basic subsistence activities consist of slash-and-burn cultivation of tuberous crops, pig husbandry, pandanus tree cultivation, gathering of wild plants, and hunting (1971:2).

The organization of the groups in Maring society is partially dependent upon population densities in local areas. In the areas of highest densities (100 persons per square mile) clan clusters are the "largest named groups with recognized territorial boundaries and with members that act together in war and in ceremonies" (1971:3). The core of each group consists of men who belong to local clans, membership being through patrilineal descent. The integration of clans into clusters is absent in the less densely settled areas, though impermanent alliances may be made for purposes of waging war between clans with adjacent territories.

Among the Marings there are three types of warring activities: nothing fights, true fights, and raids. For nothing fights and true fights the men of the opposing groups lined up on the chosen battleground as described previously. During nothing fights men stayed mostly behind their shields, emerging momentarily to taunt the enemy and display bravery, against the small bows and arrows that were used for these fracases. Nothing fights which did not escalate to true fights usually ended in negotiation and often resolved some of the conflicts at issue between the factions.

True fights, which were fought from the same basic formation as nothing fights involved a larger variety of weapons and often involved duels and close combat as well. True fights escalated from nothing fights on the agreement of the antagonists and only after both sides withdrew for two days for ritual preparation. As such wars were still fought behind fixed shields they might go on for some months at a time. True fights could also end in a negotiated settlement or a stalemate or a rout of one side by the other. A rout consisted of the victorious side pressing their fight to the settlements of the enemy, burning the houses, killing any men, women, and children not yet in flight, and destroying the gardens. This would occur when one of the sets of belligerents retreated from the battleground, or failed to show up at the field without notifying the opposing side of their intended absence.

Raids, which were rare, consisted of the men from one of the fighting groups moving in upon the settlement of the enemy by night. At dawn the houses in which the men slept were made fast and arrows and long spears were shot and poked into the houses. Men escaping through the doors were picked off—if they managed to get the doors open to begin with. Raids might end in a rout if the group attacked were small enough or might be the prelude to a rout in a true fight.

Following a rout, the members of the defeated group would either flee to the farther border of their territory and settle there or move in with kinsmen located in other groups and clan clusters. After a time members of the group might attempt to reconstitute and reclaim their lost territory. Sometimes reclamation might take place up to ten years after the rout (1971:7).

According to Vayda such wars operated in the phases: from peace without land distribution, through nothing fights, raids, true fights, routing, refuging, to peace with land distribution. Effectively the wars altered the land/man/resource balance throughout the area or between the groups contesting. Warfare was part of a phase of expansion for those groups or clan clusters which may have experienced a per capita decrease in food supplies, though this might not have reached the limit of the area's carrying capacity, or when primary forest is less available for conversion to gardens. Such a lowered ratio of primary forest would also affect the amount of game available and certainly the amount of territory within which a hunter could effectively search for game. Any of these cues or pressures might act as thresholds for aggressive behavior after which warfare might lead to an adjustment of man/resource ratios.

The beauty of Vayda's explanation lies partially in his attempt to see warfare, or the actual combat, as part of a longer, cycling process which over time continually tests, retests, and adjusts persons to available land. As he states:

. . . even if territorial conquests had been only an infrequent rather than a regular aftermath of Maring warfare for a considerable time, the warfare remained the kind that could, through an already institutionalized systemic process, lead again to the adjustment of man/resource ratios whenever demographic and ecological conditions changed sufficiently to make it appropriate for this to happen.

In the study of warfare therefore we must often look beyond the immediate events to determine the relation of warfare to the society in question. Sometimes immediate explanations may not be possible and it is only when we put our available data in a larger systemic context that we can begin to ferret out the effects of warfare within a group.

Warfare as a Way of Life: The Yanomamo
Hostility, belligerency, and warfare appear almost as constants in the Yanomamo way of life as described by Chagnon (1968a:109-159). The Yanomamo are a slash-and-burn, tropical forest people, living near the headwaters of the Orinoco River along the political boundary between Brazil and Venezuela. They represent a population of about 10,000 persons (MacCluer, Neel and Chagnon 1971:194) divided among approximately 125 villages which range in size from about 40 to 250 persons per village. The total area they occupy is about 110,000 square kilometers, with an average density of 10 persons per 100 square kilometers.

Among the Yanomamo descent is patrilineal though such links are usually weak, having a depth of only three or four generations genealogically (1968a:142-143). Generally the society is organized in terms of lineages rather than clans, the local village segments of which are corporate groups whose estate consists of women and the rights to allocate them in marriage. While in large villages a lineage segment may be composed of two or three descent groups, each making their own marital arrangements, the villages tend to be "dominated in composition by two lineages." (1968a:143). Most marriage exchanges tend to take place between the lineages of a village. However inbreeding and isolation are prevented by outside marriages, by women-stealing, and by demands on the part of stronger villages for wives from weaker communities. Also "village fission and population growth are such that third or fourth generation descendants of a man are scattered in several widely separated villages that frequently have no contacts with each other" (1968a:143).

Yanomamo warfare, as characterized by Chagnon (1968a:110), exhibits:

... smallness of scale in military operations, short duration of active hostilities, poor development of command and discipline, great reliance on stealth and surprise attacks, and a great significance of village community or local group in organizing and conducting war parties.

While the characteristics of Yanomamo warfare are in many respects similar to the characteristics of primitive warfare everywhere, they do seem to lack the ritualized "nothing" and "true" fights Vayda describes for the Marings of New Guinea.

Furthermore, as Vayda suggests was the case for the Marings, Chagnon asserts that "conflicts are not initiated or perpetuated with territorial gain as an objective or consequence" (1968a:110). Rather, Yanomamo "are obliged to adapt to a sociopolitical milieu in which members of independent villages attempt to steal each other's women" (1968a:110). Partly for this reason Chagnon adopts Harding's concept (1960:45-68) of cultural ecology which includes the existence of other sociopolitical systems as part of the environment and nature to which a people must adapt.

For Chagnon, warfare and the militant ideology of the Yanomamo serves to "preserve the sovereignty of independent villages in a milieu of chronic warfare" (1968a:112). In Chagnon's terms this is brought about by the failure of Yanomamo political institutions to control conflict within villages. This conflict produces fights which lead to the division of villages into independent and mutually hostile entities. In order to "... maximize their chances for independent political existence in this milieu, members of sovereign villages protect their autonomy by adopting an agonistic stance toward neighboring groups" (1968a:112). It would appear that the Yanomamo have learned to live by the dictum: "The best defense is a good offense." Warfare exists because there is nothing extant in Yanomamo society which can prevent its recurrence once the cycle is initiated.

While Chagnon eschews psychological explanations of warfare among the Yanomamo, he indicates that warfare is maintained in part by the institutionalization of what he terms the "waiteri complex." This complex of behavior is the display of "ferocity" by members of one social group towards another. Such a display limits the demands one village can make upon another—especially as regards the demand for women.

At the level of the social group this complex is fed by the belief that magic is often the cause of death. Death is therefore caused by one's enemies. Equally contributing to the maintenance of the "waiteri complex" is both village and tribal ethnocentrism. All other peoples are considered inferior to Yanomamo. Also among Yanomamo themselves differences between villages or social groups are exaggerated, ridiculed, and intensified.

In terms of the men, who ultimately fight the wars, "waiteri" or ferocity is encouraged from an early age in small children, as the following quotations indicate:

1. *Yanomamo boys, like all boys, fear pain and personal danger. They must be forced to tolerate it and learn to accept ferocity as a way of life (1968a:130).*

2. *Young men are competitive and attempt to show their capacity for rage, usually by temper tantrums that are ostentatious and faked (1968a:131).*

3. *Another example of the degree to which warfare and aggression are influential in the socialization process is the practice of memorizing "death speeches." Young men invent and commit to memory the words they will say in the event that they are mortally wounded (1968a:131).*

At this point in time warfare occurs because warfare exists and young men are early socialized to accept its existence and participate in it. That young men must be forced to tolerate pain and to participate in chest pounding duels initially indicates that while psychological variables may not be "sufficient" to explain the causes of war among the Yanomamo, these variables are still necessary conditions which must be fulfilled if warfare is to take place and be maintained within the society.

As regards the relation between warfare and population, Chagnon observes that warfare is not fought for territorial gain. However, warfare does have some bearing on land/man ratios as Vayda reformulated the problem in the 1971 article. In the first instance Chagnon indicates that if warfare becomes too intense people may migrate to either the periphery of the region or away from it altogether. Secondly, villages themselves move: "Clearly village mobility is marked, a reflection of the intensity of warfare in this area" (1968a:118).

By the same token village size is very important both in terms of defending oneself against aggressors and in terms of the potential for a community to divide into smaller social groups. At a level below forty people (1968a:125) a community would be too vulnerable to exist, so that members of the resulting small faction are likely to seek refuge in a larger group. Above this level smaller villages will display more "waiteri" toward larger communities in an attempt to limit the demands the larger groups may make upon them in terms of brides, etc. At the upper level larger villages, which may be in a better position to make demands upon their smaller counterparts, are more likely to divide into two or more groups through the increased likelihood of unresolvable conflict generated within the community.

Warfare, among the Yanomamo, also manages to kill people. From the demographic evidence presented (1968a:140) it appears that of a group of 240 recorded deaths (adults) warfare accounted for over 15 percent. The largest proportion of those dying by such causes were men. Lastly, through warfare the Yanomamo have been successful, as was the case with the Mundurucu, of keeping other tribes from encroaching upon their territorial area.

The evidence that Chagnon presents seems to support Vayda's assertion that warfare adjusts land/man ratios. The main difference lies in the fact that for the Marings as described by Vayda population pressure as expressed through decreases in per-capita consumables is the threshold for warring in many instances. Among the Yanomamo population pressure does not seem to work as such a device.

Raiding: Resource Instabilities Among Nomads and Hunters

One must not make the mistake of assuming that it is only sedentary societies that experience the effects of imbalances between population and resources. The balance between the number of persons in a group and their available resources remains a problem at all levels of socioeconomic integration. The pastoral nomads and herding hunters represent a level of socioeconomic and ecological integration in which the balance always seems to be extremely delicate. In fact these societies often appear to be like cybernetic systems models built in such a way that the satisfaction of the needs of some components within the total system will lead to or create an imbalance within another part or component of the system. The ability to satisfy all the demands of this way of life at the same time appears not to be possible. Raiding and warfare among such groups appear to be part of an entire cycle of momentarily correcting the imbalances.

Pastoral nomadic societies are often those for which group size and herd size and composition are closely related to warfare and raiding. In our minds it is the nomadic societies which often conjure romantic associations of warriors and warring. One is reminded of the famed cavalries of the great Ghengis Khan, the camel-riding Bedouin raiders of the Arabian deserts, and the horse-herding, buffalo-hunting Great Plains Indian societies whose life styles and warfare are usually misrepresented in movies and television where they almost always lose, fighting for unjust reasons.

Warfare seems to have been almost continuous and endemic among pastoral nomadic groups throughout the many areas of the world. In many cases such warfare is related to inherent instabilities associated with social group and animal population sizes, the carrying capacity of the environment, and, as was the case with the American Indian groups and the Mongol groups, the inherent problems of coordinating the use of the plains for the grazing of different animal populations. Among the Great Plains Indians it was often the instabilities related to the juxtaposition of the needs of the horse and the buffalo. Among the Mongols the different needs of horses and sheep led to raiding and warfare.

The Bedouin—An excellent description of the problems and intricate balancing of social and ecological forces associated with pastoral nomadism is to be found in Sweet's article on camel pastoralism in the north Arabian desert (1965: 129-152). Material from that article is recounted here.

As is the case with many pastoral nomadic societies, the Bedouin of northern Arabia do not occupy most of the area through which they roam exclusively. And, as is equally often the case, like other nomadic peoples the Bedouin are partially dependent upon the products of the other economies which interpenetrate the area through which they migrate. The summer camps at which Bedouin aggregate in their largest social groupings (the tribe) are located in the northern reaches of the Arabian peninsula close upon the outskirts of such cities as Damascus, and the more lush agricultural regions of the area.

In the interior the Bedouin share their environment with oasis cultivators, shepherd pastoralists, and other groups whose economies are based upon commerce, specialized services and crafts, camel breeding, or hunting (Sweet 1965:132, 148). It is only in the further reaches of their annual trek, the more arid deserts, that the Bedouin occupy a territory almost exclusively.

The camel, within Bedouin society, is the tool, the device used to acquire wheat, dates, and other agricultural products taken on the annual trek. Equally, the camel's ability to transport about 150 to 300 kilograms of goods per animal (Sweet 1965:133), to trek long distances on little water and utilize the sparse desert vegetation, and at times to provide transport at relative speed, has allowed the Bedouin to maintain dominance over the other users, cultivators, herders, traders, hunters, and craftsmen of his region. For a Bedouin family the camel is the fulcrum upon which survival and potential wealth are balanced against poverty and the possibility of being forced to migrate out of the context of Bedouin society itself.

Since the camel provides food (mostly milk and on rare ritual occasions meat), transport, a medium and object of exchange in barter, a potent weapon, and a means of defense, it is to the Bedouin's great advantage to increase the size of his herd as best he can. Because the lactating female provides only about one to seven liters of milk per day, there is a minimum herd size per family which must be met if the major portion of subsistence is to be drawn from camel's milk (Sweet 1965:132).

The best strategy would be to have a herd of viable females half of which would be presently providing milk and half of which would be pregnant, so as to provide milk in the future. The offspring, mainly males, could be eaten, and the females, if unwanted, could be used for barter at some future time. The number of offspring raised is important, of course, as they also are consumers of the available supply of milk.

For a family of about five persons the Bedouin might need about eighteen female camels, two baggage camels for the tent and other equipment, and several riding camels. A herd of between twenty and twenty-five animals would keep such a family well supplied and capable of meeting most needs during the annual cycle of events. Any reduction in a herd of this size would be immediately felt within the family. A loss of the females would result in smaller shares of the milk they are highly dependent upon, a loss in the riding camels in decreased mobility, and a loss of baggage animals in an increased work load on other animals. A loss of any of the camels would result in a decreased capacity to barter and obtaiñ the goods and services which are either necessary or make life in the desert regions somewhat more amenable.

Given these circumstances, Bedouin families continually attempt to maximize herd size. Any number of camels above the minimum necessary is not only an increment to wealth, status, and potential comfort, but is itself insurance, should losses occur, that there will be enough left to meet their needs. The desert, however, is a stringent environment and there are many problems, situations, and circumstances which make it very difficult to increase and maintain large herd sizes. Of course these difficulties themselves act as incentives to maintain large herds.

The first impediment Bedouin families face is the breeding rate of the camels themselves. A "female camel is bred for the first time in her sixth year, and then only once in two years produces a single offspring" (Sweet 1965:132). Under such conditions it would be very difficult to maintain in actuality the ideal previously stated of keeping half of one's herd lactating and half pregnant. Of course, the larger one's herd is the less need there is to maintain such strict proportions. Moreover, it becomes quite clear that with the slow breeding rate it would be very difficult following a loss to bring one's herd back to its previous size through breeding alone.

The second impediment is the environment itself. Desert vegetation is usually quite sparse and unevenly distributed under the best of conditions. Deserts are not places notoriously known for generous quantities of ground-water being available to plants. Most desert plants, therefore, are highly dependent upon rain to bloom and for sustained growth. Such rainfall is itself sparse and highly erratic. Desert rainfall is erratic in terms of timing, amounts, and geographic distribution. The onsets of the winter rains, with which the Bedouin tribes begin their annual trek, may vary by several weeks from one year to the next. The amount of rainfall, which determines the status of usable vegetation, also is quite variable. And finally, the fact that one or more regions of the desert received adequate or more than adequate rainfall in a given year is no indication that it will receive such amounts in the coming year.

Bedouin will attempt to maintain the largest herds possible. If they have had several years of good rainfall and pasturage and have not been heavily raided it is quite possible for them to have acquired more animals than the range could support under normal or below normal conditions. The Bedouin, as a consequence of these conditions, have no way of knowing if the herds which they have amassed in one or more seasons of their activities will be supported by the environment as they move out onto the winter ranges sometime after the rainfall.

Under such conditions those who have large fat herds today may face near starvation tomorrow. Those whose routes of migration forced them into straightened circumstances may find, through a change in rainfall and the flowering of their section of the desert, their positions greatly improved and themselves on the road to good fortune, however impermanently. As is the case with most pastoral nomadic groups, such as the horse- and sheep-herding Mongols and the horse-herding, buffalo-hunting Great Plains Indians, life is characterized by a great deal of economic instability, much of which is related to environmental/animal conditions.

Raiding between groups is a way of restocking one's dwindling capital. Among the Bedouin raiding becomes highly formalized (Sweet 1965:137) and a means of distributing survival property. Rituals of raiding and prohibitions against raiding close kin establish hierarchies in the order of priority as to who may be raided. Such priorities serve at least two other ends.

By prohibiting raids among closely related groups and nearby or adjacent tribal members, a group is thereby least likely to raid another group experiencing the same conditions as themselves. The groups closest to one's own on the route of annual migration are likely to be those with whom one shares closer ties of consanguinity than those further removed. These groups are also the most likely ones to be experiencing environmental conditions similar to those that induced the raiding in the first place.

The prohibitions against raiding close and related parties also allows for the maintenance of a certain level of stability and security. During the time a group of men from one tribal section are off on a raid, their own camp is to that extent less well defended and they are the most vulnerable to those nearest at hand. A "war of all against all" in the immediate area would result in a situation where men would be forced to guard their diminishing herds too closely and none would be free enough to replenish the dwindling stock.

Among pastoral nomads there is a relation between mobility and the ability, as well as the need, to effectuate raids. One often finds, in such societies, that wealth and mobility are incompatible. The wealthier a group is in terms of herds, or other forms of property, the less mobile they are likely to be. The less mobile a group is the harder it will be to defend, because the initiative for attack, as well as the more pressing need, is left to the more mobile, less burdened, though poorer group. Pastoral nomadic societies have often gained hegemony over the horticultural groups located within or adjacent to their routes of march for similar reasons.

The continual tension between more opulent immobility and austere mobility has been one of the prime forms of instability among pastoral nomads. When this is coupled with environmental factors which operate to randomize prosperity and to present conditions which harshly reduce herd size, then ritualized raiding appears to serve as a means of reallocating wealth and continually readjusting man/land/herd size ratios.

The same processes may be found to have been operating among the predynastic Mongol tribes of the north Asian steppes and among the posthorse Great Plains Indians. Among the Mongols prior to the ascension of Ghengis Khan, the instabilities in their forms of pastoral nomadism were focused around the differential needs, mobility, and wealth of horse- and sheep-herding groups. As with the Bedouin of the north Arabian steppes, so too the Mongol groups needed the wheat and other agricultural products of the intermittent cultivating groups within their territory as well as the agricultural products of northern China. It was to prevent such Mongol incursions that the Chinese built the Great Wall. Control of trade across the great continental trade route was another important problem among the early Mongols as it was for the early Bedouin tribes as well. Yet in both societies control of trade and its attendant increase in affluence could also be a liability. Such wealth might make one's group vulnerable to attack and yet, aside from the small store of agricultural products which crossed with the traders, such goods did little to improve one's basic ecological adjustment or balance.

Great Plains Indians—Among the horse-herding, buffalo-hunting Great Plains Indians many of the same instabilities are to be found. Such societies as represented by the Commanche, Cheyenne, Arapaho, and Sioux groups have largely been considered as hunting societies on the basis of their dependence upon the buffalo as the main form of sustenance which they hunted. However, as Wilson (1963: 355-369) demonstrates, it makes as much sense and more to consider them as postoral nomadic groups. From the standpoint of the raiding behavior present after the introduction of the horse, raiding is better understood when considered in the light of the problems that beset the Bedouin and Mongols rather than in terms of the problems that usually beset hunters.

That horses became an important focal point of Great Plains Indian culture (and, indeed, a fulcrum of much of their economic-ecological activity) is well demonstrated by Ewers in his treatise on the horse in Blackfoot Indian culture (1955: 300-301). As he states:

The fact that the horse was a grass- rather than a meat-eater (as was the dog) compelled the Indians to pay close attention to pasturage requirements. Good grass for the horses became a determining factor in the selection of campsites and the duration of occupation of those sites. When horses consumed the grass in the neighborhood of a camp, that camp had to be moved. . . . They endeavored to locate their more settled winter camps in places where the best winter forage could be found. Thus the feeding habits of the horses conditioned Blackfoot nomadism. In addition, the need to protect farflung grazing herds of horses increased the area of camps to be defended against enemy attacks.

. . . Methods of herding, hobbling, picketing, coralling, and specialized winter care were developed in attempting to solve these problems posed by the very nature of the horse itself. The daily care and breeding of sizable herds gave to the old hunting culture something of a pastoral quality unknown to the cultures of the most primitive hunting peoples.

A plentiful supply of horses was important not only for hunting and transport but as a form of wealth and other cultural purposes as well. As Mishkin indicates (1940:21-22):

. . . Differences in the size of herds were of social and economic consequence. The man with the herd of 100 horses would not necessarily have more than 20 broken horses, the number required for the average family to carry on its basic activities. But the 80 unbroken horses he owned and the insatiable desire to acquire more and more horses was not simply connected with ostentatious display or exhibitionism. The large herd was more than a symbol of the successful warrior and high rank. It meant a man could replenish his active herd from the surplus. It meant a large unbroken herd opened a new source of revenue and provided the means for operating in a new field of economic endeavor—trading.

Raiding was also, according to Mishkin, the principal means of acquiring horses (1940: 6) as the number of horses which could be acquired through natural increase did not satisfy the growing demand.

Furthermore, those areas in which the large numbers of buffalo were to be found were not the prime breeding and grazing grounds for horses. These were either to the southwest or in the lower hill regions along the continental divide. As a consequence there was always a tension between the size of herds an area could support and the number of horses an Indian family felt were adequate to meet their needs, including the social needs. To the extent that warfare provided one of the main avenues by which a man could gain standing and rank within his community and among his tribe, raiding for horses provided not only a means of reallocating a scarce good, but reinforced the Plains Indian concept of manhood; this in turn acted to stabilize the place of war and raiding within the society. Such self-cycling feedback mechanisms between raiding-manhood-social status were undoubtedly operative among the Bedouin and Mongol groups as well. There can be little doubt that warfare as a means of keeping competitors from utilizing available resources within a group's territorial boundaries was still the predominant motive for warfare on the Great Plains. The introduction of the horse made such warfare all the more compelling.

CONTACT WARS
The Iroquois and Kwakiutl Indians
Within and between preindustrial societies there are reasons for warfare beyond those of attempting to keep one's borders free of competitors for the same resources, securing land into which a community's population can expand, or achieving access to precious water in oases and grass during

periods of drought and desiccation. The advent of the European on the North American continent, for instance, changed not only the patterns of alliance between Indian groups, but the very reasons for intertribal warfare itself.

There arose among many Indian societies wars which might best be termed "contact wars." These were conflicts between Indian groups which were largely as a consequence of their contact with Europeans. This contact often resulted for the Indians in loss of homeland, increasing dependence upon trade goods, shifts in subsistence base, and the necessity of sharing once exclusive hunting territories with other groups.

Hunt (1940) has demonstrated that the Iroquois Wars of the 1640s were very much of this order. The Iroquois had become dependent upon the goods they received from the English and the Dutch in the fur trade. Yet, as their dependence upon such products as cloth, steel, iron, pottery, etc., increased, their access to available sources of fur decreased. Much of the game within the boundaries of their own territory was either hunted out or never existed in a quantity sufficient to maintain the trade at a feasible level.

Most of the furs traded did not come from one particular territory alone, but rather were gathered in large and very extensive networks of exchange which stretched from the very borders of the Arctic into the far west and northwest. Geographically the central node at which these trails came together for the exchange of grains and other cultivated produce for furs lay outside of Iroquois territory. The center of this exchange system was located in a place called Huronia, in the north central Great Lakes area, within the territorial boundaries of the Huron nation.

If a large enough and reliable enough supply of furs could not be obtained by hunting itself, neither could sufficient quantities be obtained through raiding. Raiding the canoes that travelled along the rivers, which were used as channels for communications and conduits for trade goods, netted some furs but not in great enough quantities or predictably enough to satisfy European demands. Under such conditions warfare ensued in which the Iroquois displaced the Hurons as the central collecting and dispersing point for the vast fur regions which lay beyond and above the Great Lakes.

The Iroquois were not the only Indian group for whom contact initiated conflicts. Leacock (1954) demonstrates that involvement in the fur trade eventually reoriented the entire social structure of the Montagnais-Naskapi, a tribe in the Canadian north. The changes in "hunting territory" allocation and the increase in private property must have introduced severe strains with Naskapi society and between Naskapi and bordering tribes as well. Among the Blackfoot tribes of the northern plains the fur trade and the concomitant acquisition of guns not only changed the society in many respects but also changed the ways in which wars and skirmishes were fought (Lewis 1966).

Codere (1970) on the Kwakiutl Indians of the Northwest Coast demonstrates that potlatching became intensive and consumed great quantities of property only after the advent of Europeans in the northwest.

Potlatching, or the competitive feasting and giving of presents, often involved the conspicuous destruction of blankets and other property. After contact with Europeans and the host of changes that ensued in Kwakiutl society, these feasts reached destructive proportions, which Codere came to call "fighting with property." The types of changes which took place after contact with Europeans were changes in the structure of authority which increasingly became vested in the external European communities; changes in the status structure of Kwakiutl society itself, which must partially be defined as differential access to members of the European community, who now controlled many of the vital resources; and changes as well in the relations of Kwakiutl communities to other Northwest Coast Indian groups in the area.

As an indication of the increasing intensity of potlatches, the first recorded before 1729 (Codere 1970:90) involved the distribution of fifty-five blankets, other than woolen ones, two slaves, and fifty seals for a feast. The last potlatch recorded in Codere's work (1970:91) took place in 1936 and involved 33,000 wool blankets and divers articles to the worth of another 25,000 such blankets.

Culture Contact Stability and City-state Expansion

Preindustrial agricultural societies which achieved the status of "city-state" often appear to have required more territory than they had under cultivation in and around the environs of the city itself at its inception. It may well have been that these extensive holdings were needed only secondarily for increasing agricultural acreage. Primarily they may have been required in order to absorb increases from the city's population itself. Equally such more sparsely settled land may have acted as a buffer zone between the city center and the uncontrolled periphery.

Such stably located societies had achieved, through corvée labor, a certain monumentality of architecture at the city center, and through trade and use of available resources, a certain level of wealth which to the poorer nomadic groups on the periphery may have appeared as opulence. Also, through whatever system of social stratification was operant at the time, they had achieved a certain order to their society in which the more wealthy members felt some investment in maintaining. These investments, in a beneficial social order for the wealthy, in architecture, in irrigation and involved agricultural production, are by nature permanently located and an inviting target for those less well situated at and beyond the city-state's borders. In such situations a buffer zone between the heartland and the intruders may have seemed a slight haven in a constant storm. The conquest of such external territories might seem a small price to pay for the protection they provided and for peace at home.

Some of the wealth had to be obtained from the wanderers themselves. Aside from grazing their herds, pastoral groups have acted as the transmission lines across which trade took place. As a consequence it was often necessary to allow them to move within one's borders. In such situations the sight of a standing militia might discourage whatever thoughts they may have had about making the city their permanent residence.

Furthermore, much of the economics of city-states was dependent upon the availability of trade materials, metal ores, stone, woods of various kinds, etc. As was the case with the Iroquois described earlier, a smaller but steadier and predictable quantity of trade materials is often more important for the effective operation of an economy than larger but unpredictable quantities. A standing militia could guard the trade routes whether by land or sea and if access to the goods became even more imperative such areas could be secured by conquest.

Military forces cost food and wealth, and if such a cadre were to be maintained on a permanent basis, unlike Cincinnatus who in times of emergency would trade his plow for a sword, such costs might treble. Under such conditions marginal land might have to be utilized more intensively. Such a buffer zone would no longer buffer but would now be of vital economic necessity in supporting the army its conquest created.

Warfare Technology
and Levels of
Socioeconomic Integration

It is apparent that the type of warfare fought by the Great Plains Indians, the Bedouins, the Marings of New Guinea, and the wars of the city-states are all quite different in character. Not only are the reasons why societies war subject to evolutionary change, but so too are the forms of warfare, the consequences for the participants involved, and the technology with which it is fought. The technology of warfare and its level of availability to a population will have consequences in terms of who in a society will fight as well.

Among small, egalitarian or near egalitarian band-level hunting and gathering societies, warfare often takes the form of endless interfamilial feuding. In such societies, where apart from the contenders there are not enough persons or groups with sufficient power to bring such activities to an end against the will of the contending parties, feuds may be carried on for generation after generation. Such feuds between families or bands are likely to be initiated at the occurrence of some real or imagined grievance and/or the accidental or intentional death of a member of the group whose demise is considered to be the responsibility of an opposite social group.

In nation-states members of the society have disequal opportunity to have their country declare war on their behalf. Even here the deaths of important individuals, such as the death of the Archduke Ferdinand at Sarajevo before the beginning of the First World War, are more likely to act as triggers to set in motion events which were well under way in any case. It is hardly likely that under more propitious circumstances the Archduke's assassination would have resulted in similarly catastrophic consequences. The causes of World War I lay not in his death but in the arms race which preceded it, the antagonisms produced by the competitive colonialization of Africa and Asia, and the systems of alliance between the nations of Europe which determined the distribution of national power and material resources to feed the burgeoning industrialization of Europe. Similarly, all romance aside, it is hardly likely that the abduction of Helen would have made the

Greeks war against the Trojans for ten long years if there had not been other pressing and equally irritating issues involved.

In egalitarian and rank-ordered societies too (Fried 1967: passim) the warriors would be all of the men able and competent to serve. The position of warrior or soldier as such is not a form of economic specialization and carries with it little or no military rank. Military rank in such societies is equally likely to be " . . . ephemeral, and, even more, they are contained within the patterns of kinship that are the main coordinates of group formation" (Fried 1967: 215-216). It is not until the advent of the nation-state that the military becomes a major occupation, the recruitment for which may be made by those in power relatively independent of concerns for family and kin. In societies whose mode of organization is the band or the tribe the main mode of recruitment for warfare and the organization of war parties would most likely follow the kinship structure of the society itself.

Since there is little specialization in terms of warfare as an occupation in such societies, there is usually equally little production for warfare either. By and large the weapons of war may be the weapons of the hunt, though perhaps more decorative in adornment. In many cases it is likely that all men make their own weapons. Furthermore in such societies there is little likelihood that there will be a special diversion of subsistence goods for the maintenance of warfare. Often warfare occurs only during the slack agricultural season or during the period when the hunt is least productive.

WARFARE AND WEAPONRY
With the increasing complexity of societies and the growth of agricultural and industrial production warfare itself assumes more of the character of an industry requiring more and more of the resources of the society. Production of weaponry and armor itself becomes a specialization and finally an industry. As time passes the maintenance and equipping of a militia requires the diversion of more and more of a society's production. Butter must finally give way to guns.

Beyond this the type of weaponry employed in any age and the technology available to produce and support it is partly determined by who among the men of a society would use it. The weapons of the Great Plains Indians and the Marings of New Guinea were hardly different than the weapons of hunting and were available through self-manufacture to all men. In addition as opposed to metal ores the materials out of which weapons were made were distributed more uniformly throughout forest and plain.

The advent of bronze and the cost incurred in the manufacture of bronze weaponry put such weapons beyond the reach of most peasant agriculturalists. Furthermore it required the acquisition of ore sites often far beyond the boundaries of the nation seeking such material. Specialists were required as well for the manufacture of weapons. The later use of and spread of iron and steel, though it remained in the hands of specialists for manufacture, democratized the availability of metal weapons partly through the reduced costs of obtaining ores.

With the invention of the iron stirrup the peasant army was once again out of business, since poorly armed cadres of infantry were an inadequate weapon against a horse-mounted cavalry of armored knights. As such armor required a great deal of specialization and time in manufacture, only a small portion of the social order could afford to maintain smithies for its production. Horse armor was effectively a weapon of the aristocracy.

In England the acceptance of the crossbow and the development of the longbow with which English troops cut down the "flower of French chivalry" at the battle of Agincourt in 1415 once again gave the peasant armed infantry supremacy over the armored cavalry. The use of the crossbow, the halberd and pike likewise gave the Swiss supremacy over cavalry. Furthermore these weapons could be produced from materials more readily available and at a greatly reduced cost.

The development of handguns from the arquebus and the later use of artillery once again put weaponry beyond the reach of the individual. Producing artillery pieces in sufficient enough quantities is a manufacturer's art and its deployment required a large number of horses and men both to operate the weapon and to bring up and maintain sufficient gunpowder and the very heavy shells then employed. From that time forward the weaponry of war has remained largely in the hands of government and the industries necessary to manufacture it. The American Civil War may in some respects have been the first war in which industry played such a telling part, for surely it was the heavy industry of the North and its adjunct railways which played the greatest part in depriving the South of victory.

In band-level societies the primary objectives of war are likely to be personal, represented either in terms of a specific person or a specific and usually small social group. Only secondarily, if at all, are the objectives likely to be economic and impersonal. Tactics themselves will be dictated as the occasions arise and the fighting takes place mostly in skirmishes which are usually short lived. In industrial states, on the other hand, targets or objectives are hardly ever likely to be immediately personal. They are more likely to be military (strategic geographic positions) or economic (production complexes) or both. Warfare is likely to be prolonged and individual skirmishes between troops, rather than being the whole of a battle, are likely to be a part of larger tactical designs and considerations.

Often, as is the case with aerial bombardment and artillery fire, there is little or no direct contact between the enemies. In those cases where hand-to-hand combat may occur it is usually either the result of some mismanagement of the tactical plan or the result of a flaw in the tactical design itself. Modern battles and bureaucratic wars are much too costly in terms of men and equipment to leave the outcome in the hands of such unpredictable factors as personal strength, endurance, or willpower.

In this respect, guerilla wars may be the "Achilles' heel" of a bureaucratized military force. The experience of the French in Algiers and Vietnam, the British in the Carolinas during the American Revolution, and the United States in Vietnam, indicates that under certain circumstances bureaucratized forces have limited flexibility in responding to prolonged partisan conflicts. Bureaucratic armies are best employed in unrestricted warfare where a territory becomes occupied by one side or another. In the guerilla operations of the "Peasant Wars of the Twentieth Century," (as Eric Wolf titles his book: 1969) the contenders may be occupying the same territory. Any attempt to utilize the superior technology of the bureaucratized force often ends by being as damaging to one side as to the other. It is very likely that such recent experiences as the Vietnam War and Algiers will produce changes in the technology of war and the operations by which such events take place. What these changes will be remains to be seen and will require the next such war for their exhibition.

Summary and Afterthoughts

THEORY AND DEFINITION

Along with the "great American novel" the final treatise on the relations between man, society, and the wars he commits himself to fighting has yet to be written. It follows ony, therefore, that this treatise on the subject is not yet it. There are a good many issues yet to settle.

Scientific work often raises as many questions as it provides answers. The dissatisfactions we feel with the answers we receive form our motivation to research further, to create ever closer successive approximations of reality. It is important then that we conclude this work not by simply reviewing what it is we already know. Rather it is important to ask questions about how we can come to know what is yet to be dealt with and what the consequences of that knowledge might be for our theory of man and warfare. Equally, as ethnographers it is important for us to ask questions about what kinds of data we may have yet to examine in relation to knowing about warfare.

Whether or not one accepts war as being as old as mankind is partially a matter of how one defines warfare. If within the framework of the definition are included those sporadic acts of violence that erupt into and maintain feuds between families or the small egalitarian bands that lack definite leadership, which must have been characteristic of social groups of early man, then warfare is indeed as old as mankind itself. At this point it would be necessary to invoke the *caveat* that, while we might agree that men may have always warred, there is no evidence to confirm the assertion that *all* men have warred. On the other hand, if one insists that acts of hostility, in order to be defined as acts of war, must exhibit some form of leadership and some planning, as well as the use of armed force, then feuds as such could not be included within the domain of the concept of warfare. Warfare, thereby, would be seen as a social activity whose genesis arose later in time than the development of the species itself. It would have had to have been the result of activities or conditions related to the procession of man's sociocultural evolution.

The problem of definition, which pervades all of the sciences, in relation to all scientific endeavors, is not an inconsequential matter. The particular definition of warfare used makes it possible, as noted above, for the investigator to select certain phenomena as within his domain of inquiry and to reject other material. All definitions are equally acts of exclusion as well as acts of inclusion. The logic of sets works in such a manner that it provides the scientist with a certain economy in his investigation. But equally, it places upon him the responsibility of determining *a priori* what the goals of his investigation will be and for setting boundaries to the concepts he employs, boundaries which will fairly and equitably exhaust the material under investigation.

Such a set of statements or definitions of the subject matter could be called a "theory of warfare." A theory provides the investigator with a framework of assertions from which he can initiate an investigation while, at the same time, it still allows him the freedom to disconfirm the initial propositions with which he began, if he can. One of the goals of social science, as with all the sciences, is to achieve a "general theory" of human behavior from which the investigation of particular human activities, such as warfare, might proceed. As yet the social sciences have not achieved their equivalents to Newton's Laws of Motion or Einstein's Theory of Relativity. Until such time as most social scientists can agree upon a general theory, the study of warfare, as with the study of any other human endeavor, for that matter, will remain in such a state that each investigator will be required to ask of himself, prior to his investigation, the very fundamental questions related to what he considers human life to be about.

Evolutionary Theory
If his approach to war is from an evolutionary perspective the definition will have to be broad enough to permit the initial examination of data at many different levels of socioeconomic integration. In this respect Fried's relatively broad rendering of Quincy Wright's definition (Wright 1965) "the . . . condition which . . . permits two or more hostile groups to carry on a conflict by armed force," (Fried 1967: 100) might suffice. Within the context of this relatively broad definition the investigator will still have to ask of himself such questions as: "Is leadership essential to the conduct of war?" "If so, what constitutes leadership?" "Of what importance is planning?" "What role does the acquisition of territory play in the nature of war?" Even more fundamentally he will have to face answering such questions as: "Is warfare an activity confined to members of the human species alone?" "If not, is the basis for warfare common to all sexually reproducing animals?" "If solely human is warfare panhuman?" "Is warfare only evolutionary in the

forms which it takes and the various instruments and technologies with which it is pursued?" or, "Is warfare a part and product of the entire panorama of sociocultural evolution?"

These are important questions which will remain the proverbial objects of scientific discourse until such time as we have developed a general theory of human behavior which will provide us with a set or sets of paradigms with which to initiate our investigations. Since these questions cannot be answered in relation to the paradigms of a general theory they can only be dealt with in relation to the possible consequences that the answers might have on the conduct of research itself.

For instance the biological ethologists, as represented by Lorenz, look for the rudiments of warfare in animal behavior and accept as evidence any act of aggression as meaningful to their case. When this approach is applied to the study of human behavior such a broad definition leaves the human sciences in such a definitional state that it is not possible to discriminate between the act of shooing a salesman away from the front door and the Second World War. This state of affairs is a consequence of the nature of scientific definitions.

A further consequence of accepting any act of aggression as consonant with the definition of war is to affirm the Hobbesian world view of man living in the condition of the "war of all against all." The scientist would not have to ask what conditions call forth war since the sum total of man's aggressive behavior would mean that man lived in a perpetual state of war. The irony of this position is that the ethologists, who are almost by definition concerned with the process of evolution, are saying, in effect, that warfare itself is not evolutionary. What is evolutionary in this case is not war but the forms it takes, the behaviors and displays it exhibits.

It may appear useful, to others, to separate the dismissal of salesmen from the front door from the types of hostilities generated between nations. In terms of an evolutionary perspective one needs to determine which aggressive acts are related to one's own concepts of warfare and which aggressive acts are not. This is a minimally essential conditon for a theory of the evolution of warfare.

The various definitions of warfare that the scientist might employ will have consequences for the way in which he will see the relation between warfare and society as well as determining which acts of violence will be included or excluded by the definition. But it is equally true that the initial premises of his social theory will have consequences for the ways in which he defines war and for the ways in which he will realize the relations between warfare and the social order. The ways in which the investigator deals with such questions as: "What is human about being human?" "What constitutes a social group?" "What are the relations between social groups, however defined, and their resource base?" and "In what way are social groups or the activities of social groups purposeful?" will affect an investigator's view of the relation between society and any one of its myriad institutions and activities, including warfare.

Structural-Functional Theory

For instance, one might start with the major premises of the "structural-functional" school. These are: (1) societies are integrated wholes whose (2) institutions are interrelated and adjusted to each other through (3) a process of functional integration whose main purpose is (4) the maintenance of social equilibrium which (5) individuals as well as groups work to achieve and maintain. Under such conditions the investigator is expected to demonstrate, relative to any institution he studies, the ways in which this integration is achieved and the way the institution operates so as to maintain equilibrium. Equally he is expected to uncover those underlying patterns of relations which constitute the structure of society. Such a view of the social order is a static one and one which does not incorporate any propositions about growth and change within the framework of its basic premises.

Given these premises and concerns, the number of options available for viewing the relation of warfare to society are extremely limited. Warfare may be either functional or dysfunctional. It either contributes to the maintenance of social cohesion or it does not. If warfare does not contribute to the maintenance of the social order then warfare as a subject matter falls largely outside the purview of the major premises of functional theory. The concept of dysfunction as used by members of the structural-functional school does not in itself constitute an adequate theory of social change. For them dysfunction means only that an institution or activity is not contributing to the maintenance of social cohesion. Dysfunctional activities may, as it were, have little or no effect on the social order at all, and are therefore not necessarily agents of change.

Under such conditions the investigator may conclude that warfare operates to maintain social cohesion or he may abandon the structural-functional position altogether. Another option is to view warfare in terms of a set of contingencies external to the society itself. Here the investigator would talk about warfare in relation to the movement of technologies and ideologies between societies through the processes of diffusion and acculturation. Such an approach tends to avoid issues related to what wars are about and how they are generated and deals mainly with what wars do to a society and how, if at all, they are maintained.

One should not be misled into believing that wherever the word "functional" or "function" is used in an article or book the authors are, by such a fact, structural-functionalists. Furthermore one cannot assume that the concept of function has no place within the realm of the social sciences because it is utilized by structural-functionalists. To do so would be to accomplish the proverbial feat of "throwing the baby out with the bath water." It is a very respectable scientific occupation to be engaged in answering questions about how things work. The only stipulation that need be made here would be that explanations should be couched within the context of a theoretical framework which would account for the occurrence of internal change and growth as well as changes wrought through external sources. Such a criterion for social theory must be regarded as minimally essential in that change is an ever-present product of social processes.

Systems Theory

An example of an anthropologist's work in which the concepts of function and equilibrium are used in a nonstatic way is Vayda's explanation of warfare among the Marings of New Guinea. To couch Vayda's explanation in general systems theory terms, warfare operates among the Marings as a response to negative feedback, to redress the disequilibrated balance between a social group's size, the subsistence it requires, and the land available on which such resources must be cultivated. To maintain the proper balance, group size and available land resources must fluctuate relative to each other and relative to a given technology which allows them to produce so much food per acre. Any activity which would effectively increase the size of the population or decrease the amount of land available below a certain point might produce warfare.

It is possible to think of a number of inputs to the system which could create this effect. For instance, increased fertility for the tribe or clan, decreased mortality and increased in-migration of relatives from other clans would all increase the population size relative to available resources. On the other hand loss of land through invasion, poor land management resulting in massive erosion, and suchlike causes might lead to less land for utilization for the same amount of people. Events which would also affect production itself, and not immediately the size of the group or the available land, might have similar results. Such occurrences might be a succession of poor growing seasons due to changes in edaphic conditions, or a decline in soil fertility, or even such events as a plague of insect pests upon the food crops. Any one or any combination of such events could lead to a situation whereby it would be necessary to redress the balance between the size of the group and its available land resources.

In general systems theory such a set of relations and associated conditions as Maring warfare exhibits would be called an open system. Open systems, as characterized by Buckley (1967:52-53) are those which meet the following criteria:

1. *Whose characteristic features depend on certain internal parameters or criterion variables remaining within certain limits;*

2. *Whose organization has developed a selective sensitivity, or mapped relationship, to environmental things or events of relevance to these criterion variables;*

3. *Whose sensory .apparatus is able to distinguish any deviations of the systems' internal states and/or overt behavior from goal-states defined in terms of the criterion variables;*

4. *Such that feedback of this "mismatch" information into the system's behavior-directing centers reduces (in the case of negative feedback) or increases (in the case of positive feedback) the deviation of the system from its goal-states or criterion limits.*

More simply put, an "open-system" is one in which dissimilar events may lead to the same results. An example of a relatively closed system is a watch or timepiece. A watch has one external source of energy, the "main stem," and it will operate at a steady level only so long as the mainspring's tension is kept above certain limits through winding the stem (Berrien 1968:16). Unlike a watch the Maring resource system can be affected at many different points.

Conflict and Psychology Theory
Dahrendorf's position is one which must be regarded as dynamic as well. If one accepts his initial premise that conflict is central to the social system and is the machinery by which societies change, grow, and pass away, one would not be inclined to separate wars into functional and dysfunctional categories. Rather one would regard war as being involved with the very process of social growth itself and as universally possible, within the framework of each human society, as are the embedded conflicts which generate such war. Warfare would be regarded as universal on the grounds that conflict is universally inherent in all forms of human social organization.

Viewed in this way the concepts of Freud, Holloway, and Dahrendorf are compatible. Holloway and Freud see war as the result of frustrations and thwarted aggressive tendencies which arise within mankind in social groups. Freud relates such acts to social control of the *id*—the energy generator, as it

49

were, within man. Holloway looks for explanations of warfare in terms of social causation but sees it related to the cortical complexity and intellectual capacity that man has achieved.

Obviously whatever biological and psychological mechanisms there are which underlie warfare they would have to be universal to all of the members of the species. This, in essence, is part of what is meant by the concept of the "psychic unity" of mankind. To the extent that the proposition is accepted that the underlying bio-psychological mechanisms are universal to mankind one would have to accept one of two possible propositions about the relationship of warfare to society. This is required in that warfare unlike "psychic unity" is by no means universal. In the first instance one could assert that warfare has unique social causation and thereby deny the relevance of any underlying biological and/or psychological mechanisms. On the other hand one could assert the proposition that warfare has psychic causes, but that these psychic conditions have not as yet been manifested in those societies which have not as yet experienced war.

This latter position allows the investigator, as Sorokin once said of another set of assertions (Sorokin 1956) the opportunity to cash a check upon a bank that hasn't been built yet. Many of the societies that have not experienced war have passed out of existence, as have many of those which have experienced war. For those that may be left it seems unfair to wait until such conditions are created as would make any other response impossible.

The only fair test would be one in which the group could offer alternative responses besides war and feel that these responses would be effective. Under situations in which the enemy had given every indication that they would proceed with systematic extinction of the group and/or expropriate their homeland in any case, the group would have little or nothing left to lose and only one response possible. Equally, pushing an animal beyond the boundaries of its normally expressed social behavior is hardly a fair test of its aggressive tendencies either.

At best, it may be fair to say that it is highly probable that all wars have some psychic effect. One of the possible effects is that societies which have warred and not found the conditions too intolerable may come to accept warfare as a solution to problems other than the ones for which they initially went to war. It might be said that such societies had developed a "psychological" dependence upon warfare as a means of solving social problems.

Even here, however, the explanation in terms of psychological dependence is the least interesting of two possible statements about a society's initiating a war. The other order of explanation would deal with those social problems which warfare was intended to solve. Warfare would, in these terms, still be viewed as a sociocultural phenomenon.

ETHNOGRAPHY AND THE EVIDENCE OF WARFARE:
SOME SPECULATIONS

Putting aside the question of definition and its relation to theory, it may be worthwhile, in concluding, to offer some speculations on the following situation. Suppose for a moment that an anthropologist is engaged in an ethnographic study of a society with a preindustrial technology which has no written record or historical source materials available. If the society had been pacified since the coming of a colonial administration what clues could the anthropologist look for within the context of the culture itself to indicate that this particular society had been involved in endemic or nearly endemic warfare in its past? Essentially the question is to determine what the consequences of relatively frequent war might be or have been for a society.

This framework for the question is not an idle one. Many of the present societies with preindustrial technologies no longer war. Warfare between indigenous or aboriginal groups largely ended following the period of European expansion and colonialism. While the early contacts between Europeans may have touched off whole series of contact wars the general trend was and has been toward pacification. Warfare, between active groups, was too costly in men and material and too disruptive of the flow of local resources for colonial administrators to allow.

It is interesting to note that those areas of the world in which indigenous wars are still being fought are precisely those areas which are still marginal to the economic interests of industrial nations. The interior highlands of New Guinea and much of the Amazon area of South America today represent examples of the marginal areas where native wars are still being fought. Given the industrial world's need for increased resources and an elaborate technology with which to secure such resources these areas will be pacified as well within the near future. Shortly the only remnants of indigenous warfare which the ethnologist will have at his disposal will be those descriptions already captured in the ethnographic record and those remaining aspects of the behavior of aboriginal societies which we can infer had something to do with warfare in the past.

How might one know, therefore, from the study of a society's present-day culture whether or not the precursors of the group were heavily involved in warfare? There is not enough time or space to suggest all of the possible lines of evidence that an ethnographer might search out. Rather the attempt here is to be somewhat speculative as well as necessarily incomplete.

Spatial Organization
With respect to societies involved in horticultural subsistence practices, evidence that might suggest that the group had been involved in warfare on

their own home ground would be the shape of the village itself. Where a society or community must prepare for the defense of their home ground there is the possibility that they might erect fences, barricades, or earthworks around the living sites. They might equally organize the dwelling sites into geometric patterns such as circles or squares which they feel offer some defensive advantage for their type of warfare.

Pastoral nomadic groups and hunting bands on the other hand, if sufficiently forewarned, can disperse and move from under an imminent attack. During those periods when such groups are dispersed throughout their territories or along their routes of march in the smallest aggregates their cultural mores and subsistence practices permit they are, in terms of sheer numbers for defense, the most vulnerable. Such vulnerability is offset by the fact that small groups are often capable of greater mobility than large groups. Spreading out through a territory also reduces the probability of attacks being delivered for each group. During periods when subsistence activities demand small less defensible groups, mobility and dispersion may be the best defensive tactics the society possesses.

In horticultural, and agricultural societies as well, movement is not an answer to the problems of defense. Unlike pastoral nomads their resources tend, at least during the growing season, to remain fixed. Village form and fortifications may provide a partial answer. Another aid would definitely be the development of alliances with neighboring communities and, if possible, the development of forms of social organization which might operate to concentrate and maintain men within the local area. Where defensive wars had been fought one might find a situation in which residence in the community is virilocal and members of the community attempt to encourage other men to join the community.

Unilineal Structure

Such a solution is not without attendant problems. The Otterbeins (Otterbein, K. F. and C. S. Otterbein 1965: 1470-1482; Otterbein 1968: 277-289; Otterbein 1970: 1-165) establish in their cross-cultural surveys of wars and feuds that at the lower levels of political integration the presence of fraternal interest groups within the organization of the society is related to the presence of feuding. It may be that in order to solve their defensive problems such societies create the conditions where the various interest groups which divide the men of the community each receive enough support to initiate and maintain these conflicts in the form of feuds. The presence of age grades, men's clubs, men's houses, and other forms of fraternal activity may also be important clues for the ethnographer to weigh in the balance.

Matrilocal, matrilineal societies would evidence much lower indices of feuding than would patrilocal, patrilineal groups. This would be the result of the "structural condition which results in the scattering of related males over a large area; thus, it is difficult for them to support each other's interests" (Otterbein and Otterbein 1965: 1472; Otterbein 1968: 279). While matrilocal societies might not give positive evidence of a high intensity of internal feuds one cannot adduce from this condition that they are likely to be any less warlike than their patrilocal patrilineal counterparts.

Indeed a case can be made to support the hypothesis that matrilocality, matrilineality may have been the result of warfaring activities for some groups. Within matrilocal groups women form the stable core of the social group in whose presence is invested the continuity of property, the succession of men to offices and titles, and the continuance of the group itself. Women may form this stable, predictable core under conditions in which it is not possible for men to do so. One of those possible conditions in which men would not be as predictably certain and available to the group as the women would be when the men of the society were engaged in fighting extensive wars beyond the boundaries of their communal locations. Such wars might be offensive wars rather than defensive ones.

In terms of the ethnographic evidence the men of the Nayar of the Kerala area of India often were involved in wars beyond their home ground. Often too they enlisted in the ranks of external armies as mercenaries. The Iroquois after the 1640s were engaged in extensive wars which often took the men beyond the boundaries of their communities for long periods of time. And, one might wonder what all the Greek women were doing during the ten long years their men were off fighting the Trojan Wars. Matrilineality is no indication that a society is more peaceful than another which exhibits different modes of social organization.

Intensive Productivity

Preparation for defensive warfare might in horticultural societies have far-reaching effects upon the group's productivity as well as upon its organization. The need to maintain defensible-size populations within a community area might be a sufficient cause to move the group toward more intensive systems of cultivation. Within extensive horticultural systems one means of lowering the probability of any one family being hit would be to distribute all families individually over the entire domain of the community. Such a distribution of persons does not allow for any economies of scale with regard to the use of labor. Under such conditions older couples whose children had moved into their own subsistence niches would be seriously dis-advantaged as would a young married couple with many young children. Intermediate aggregations of population solve the problem of labor but defensively may be much less strategic. The concentration of families within one locale allows for a greater defensive posture but may provide more labor than the original system of cultivation demanded. Being stably located in an area for defense may also initiate sufficient environmental deterioration to require intensification of cultivation.

One possible solution to this problem short of concentration of populations is to conceal the location of the residence sites from all but the most friendly communities. This is what the Yanomamo do. Village sites would therefore have to be fairly far removed from each other to make concealment even partially effective. As in the case of the Yanomamo, the entire village could maintain a level of readiness so as to be able to abandon a village site if an overwhelming attack were suspected. The effect of this would be to distribute village groups in small concentrations over much of the entire domain of the tribe or ethnic group. In a tropical forest setting where forest resources are randomly distributed and where there is a high diversity of available plant material such a dispersed network may operate as an advantageous means of tapping the available resources.

Ritual and Myth

A group could also overcome their need for defensive barricades to the degree that they and their combatants were able to ritualize warfare between them. If wars are only fought after the initiation of a ceremony such rites can act as a signal to nearby communities to prepare for attack. Also contending communities in the area could ritualize the operations of warfare such that they would only be fought on specified fields designated for battle. Essentially this is the system utilized by the Marings and only when the battle moved heavily in favor of one group would there be an expectation of an attack upon the residence sites.

Wars and their related activities may be preserved in the myths of a society. This seems like a self-evident proposition. Wars, even in societies where they are fairly endemic, are not likely to become so usual as to be taken wholly as a matter of course. Homer's *Iliad* and *Odyssey* are excellent examples of warfare being preserved for the instruction of oncoming generations. Myths are not likely to provide clues that will allow the investigator to assess the frequency or the degree to which warfare was endemic in a given society.

The actual rendering of specific wars in the myths and tales of a people is not the only aspect of myths which may provide the ethnographer with clues to warfare in the past. Myths may also contain distillations of concepts of personhood which are qualities related to warfare activities. The qualities of personhood that a social group idealizes may also provide clues to previous warfare. Valor in the face of adversity, the ability to aggressively seize opportunities, stoicism in the face of pain and loss are characteristics which a society may wish to inculcate in its offspring. Often they use tales and myths to render these concepts more vivid. There are problems, however, in interpreting such concepts of personhood solely in relation to warfare.

We cannot assume that a society which requires more bravery, aggressiveness, stoicism, and so on of its men is necessarily more warlike than one which operates in terms of less intense exhibitions of such characteristics. Liebig's Law of the Minima may operate in this area of behavior as well as in others. Liebig's Law states that an organism or group of organisms responds and adapts to the minimum conditions available for its survival and not the maximum. Given this any society that ever fought a war even once might inculcate in its offspring those attributes of personhood which they feel will increase the probability of the offspring's survival should another such situation arise even in the remote future.

Another problem is that these attributes of personhood may persist in a society for reasons other than their possible support for warlike activities. Within the framework of our concepts of our modern economy, economic transactions are often couched in the metaphor of battle. The attributes of the soldier are often seen as not unbefitting an entrepreneur. Such transactions are often "engaged in," the transactions themselves are often described as having been won or lost, and the character of the adversary is often described in terms befitting the description of an enemy warrior. It is also not entirely clear that the only measure of personal satisfaction gained is measurable in the amount of monetary return captured in the exchange.

Social Darwinism, which was very much in vogue as an ideology during the rise and florescence of American capitalism, and which is still the philosophy some economists and business leaders utilize in describing the virtues of the capitalist system, tends to view the engagement in the marketplace as a life and death struggle. To the victors go survival and the perpetuation of their ideology. Monetary return is only an indication of the potential for survivorship. The perpetuation of the warrior concept of manhood in our society may have important implications for more than just maintaining a state of preparedness for warfare itself. Indeed it may be woven into the fabric of our economic life as well. If such a condition prevails in our society it is not too difficult to imagine that the ideal of the warrior might be perpetuated in other societies for similar and even for some disparate reasons.

The conceptions of the warrior are often enacted within a society in the play of children and in the competitions between its young men. Such play and training may serve as an indicator of warring activities as well. It will usually be the case that children play at war in terms of the modes of the dominant technology with which it is fought in that society. So children of the Yanomamo may use toy bows and arrows and spears to spear insects and animals and engage in mock chest pounding duels (Chagnon 1968b: 113-117) mimicking their future role as warriors. In our society children play with toy guns and with replicas of the types of weapons men envision as possibly being utilized in wars of the future. As with the Yanomamo, the battles they reenact are renderings made available through the dominant modes of communication available to them. In Yanomamo society these would be stories, myths, and direct experience. In American society the source of battle plans may be movies and television.

It is possible that further clues to the previous presence of warfare in a society may be found in some of the rituals of the group. Elaborate funerary rites may have been connected with the presence of warfare in the past. Many of the more intensely warfaring groups of New Guinea and South America as well as the Ibans, Kayahs, Kenyahs, and Muruts of Sarawak, Borneo, possessed elaborate funeral rituals. In some of the South American and New Guinea groups such rites sometimes involved endocannabalism and elaborate preparations of the corpse. There has not as yet been a cross-cultural survey to determine the relation between warfare and the degree of elaboration evidenced in the ethnographic literature for burial and memorial services. The sentiment elegantly expressed by the hero of the motion picture, *The Americanization of Emily*, Lieutenant Charles E. Madison, that "Wars are perpetuated by widows weeping over graves," may contain more than a small grain of truth. To the extent that a society honors its war dead and insists that they shall not have died in vain it may seek war as a solution to political problems it might otherwise have attempted to solve by more peaceful means.

It would appear that there are no certain indices or clues to a society's warring past which cannot be interpreted in other ways. As with many other aspects of the study of society and culture the best evidence may be a lot of it, and a lot of it from as many various areas of life itself as it is possible to gather.

References Cited

Angell, Robert C. 1965. The sociology of human conflict. In *The nature of human conflict*. E. B. McNeil, ed. Englewood Cliffs, N.J.: Prentice-Hall.

Appell, George N. 1966. Personal communication.

Ardrey, Robert. 1971. *The territorial imperative*. New York: Dell Publishing Co.

Bateson, Gregory. 1967. *Naven*. Stanford, Calif.: Stanford University Press.

Berrien, F. K. 1968. *General and social systems*. New Brunswick, N.J.: Rutgers University Press.

Bogue, Donald J. 1969. *Principles of demography*. New York: John Wiley and Sons.

Books in print. Volume Two: Titles and publishers. 1971. New York: R. R. Bowker Co.

Brown, Dee. 1972. *Bury my heart at Wounded Knee*. New York: Bantam Books.

Buckley, W. F. 1967. *Sociology and modern systems theory*. Englewood Cliffs, N.J.: Prentice-Hall.

Chagnon, Napoleon A. 1968a. Yanomamo social organization and warfare. In *War: The anthropology of armed conflict and aggression*. M. Fried, M. Harris, and R. Murphy, eds. New York: Natural History Press. 1968b.

_____. 1968b. *Yanomamo: The fierce people:*New York: Holt, Rinehart and Winston.

Chomsky, Noam. 1970. Linguistic theory. In *Readings in applied transformational grammar*. M. Lester, ed., pp. 51-60. New York: Holt, Rinehart and Winston.

Codere, Helen. 1970. *Fighting with property*. Monograph of the American Ethnological Society 18. Seattle, Wash.: University of Washington Press.

Coser, Lewis A. 1956. *The functions of social conflict*. New York: Free Press.

Dahrendorf, R. 1959. *Class and class conflict in industrial society*. Stanford, Calif.: Stanford University Press.

_____. 1967. *Conflict after class: New perspectives on the theory of social and political conflicts*. London: Longmans.

_____ . 1968. *Essays in the theory of society*. Stanford, Calif.: Stanford University Press.

Divale, William T. 1970. An explanation for primitive warfare: population control and the significance of primitive sex ratios. *The New Scholars,* Fall, 1970: 173-92.

Ewers, John C. 1955. *The horse in Blackfoot Indian culture.* Smithsonian Institution, Bureau of American Ethnology, Bulletin 159. Washington, D.C.: Government Printing Office.

Fried, M. H. 1967. *The evolution of political society.* New York: Random House.

Goodenough, Ward H. 1970. *Description and comparison in cultural anthropology.* Chicago: Aldine Publishing Co.

Gorer, Geoffrey. 1968. Man has no "killer" instinct. In *Man and aggression.* M. F. Ashley Montagu, ed. New York: Oxford University Press.

Harding, Thomas. 1960. Adaptation and stability. In *Evolution and culture.* Marshall D. Sahlins and Elmar R. Service, eds. Ann Arbor: University of Michigan Press.

Holloway, Ralph L., Jr. 1968. Human aggression: The need for a species-specific framework. In *War: The anthropology of armed conflict and aggression.* M. Fried, M. Harris, and R. Murphy, eds. New York: Natural History Press.

Hunt, George T. 1940. *The wars of the Iroquois.* Madison: University of Wisconsin Press.

Kammeyer, K. C. 1969. *Population studies.* New York: Rand McNally.

Langer, William L. 1972. Checks on population growth: 1750-1850. *Scientific American* 226(2): 92-99.

Leacock, Eleanor. 1954. *The Montagnais "hunting territory" and the fur trade.* Memoirs of the American Anthropological Association, no. 78.

Lewis, Oscar. 1966. *The effects of white contact upon Blackfoot culture.* Monograph of the American Ethnological Society, 6. Seattle, Wash.: University of Washington Press.

Lorenz, Konrad. 1970. *On aggression.* New York: Bantam Books.

MacCluer, J. W., J. V. Neel, and N. A. Chagnon. 1971. Demographic structure of a primitive population: A simulation. *American Journal of Physical Anthropology* 35: 193-208.

McNeil, E. B. 1965 *The nature of human conflict.* Englewood Cliffs, N. J.: Prentice-Hall.

Mishkin, Bernard. 1940. *Rank and warfare among the Plains Indians.* Monograph of the American Ethnological Society, 3. Seattle, Wash.: University of Washington Press.

Morris, Desmond. 1969. *The human zoo.* New York: McGraw-Hill Book Co.

Murphy, Robert F. 1957. Intergroup hostility and social cohesion. *American Anthropologist* 59: 1018-35.

———. 1971. *The dialectics of social life.* New York: Basic Books.

Otterbein, K. F. 1968. Internal war: A cross-cultural study. *American Anthropologist* 70: 277-89.

———. 1970. *The evolution of war.* New York: HRAF Press.

Otterbein, K. F., and C. S. Otterbein. 1965. An eye for an eye, and a tooth for a tooth: A cross-cultural study of feuding. *American Anthropologist* 67:1470-82.

Sahlins, Marshall. 1972. *Stone Age economics.* Chicago: Aldine-Atherton.

Sorokin, P. A. 1956. *Fads and foibles in modern sociology and related sciences.* Chicago: H. Regnery Co.

Sweet, Louise E. 1965. Camel pastoralism in North Arabia and the minimal camping unit. In *Man, culture and animals.* A. Leeds and A. P. Vayda, eds. Washington, D.C.: American Association for the Advancement of Science, Publication No. 78.

Turney-High, H. H. 1971. *Primitive war: Its practice and concepts.* Columbia, S. C.: University of South Carolina Press.

Vayda, A. P. 1960. *Maori warfare.* Polynesian Society Maori Monographs No. 2, Wellington, N.Z.

———. 1961. Expansion and warfare among swidden agriculturalists. *American Anthropologist* 63: 346-58.

———. 1967. Research on the functions of primitive war. Peace Research Society (International) *Papers* 7: 133-38

———. 1968. Hypotheses about functions of war. In *War: The anthropology of armed conflict and aggression.* M. Fried, M. Harris; and R. Murphy, eds. New York: Natural History Press.

———. 1970. Maoris and muskets in New Zealand: Disruption of a war system. *Political Science Quarterly* 85: 560-84.

———. 1971. Phases of the process of war and peace among the Marings of New Guinea. *Oceania* 42(1): 1-24.

Vayda, A. P. 1960. *Maori warfare.* Wellington, N.Z.: Polynesian Society Maori Monographs No. 2.

Williams, Thomas R. 1965. *The Dusun: A North Borneo society.* New York: Holt, Rinehart and Winston.

Wilson, H. Clyde. 1963. An inquiry into the nature of Plains Indian cultural development. *American Anthropologist* 65: 355-69.

Wolf, Eric R. 1969. *Peasant wars of the twentieth century.* New York: Harper and Row.

Wright, Quincy. 1965. *A study of war.* 2nd ed. Chicago: University of Chicago Press.

FURTHER REFERENCES OF INTEREST ON WARFARE

Andrzejewski, Stanislaw. 1954. *Military organization and society*. London: Routledge.

Bateson, Gregory. 1946. The pattern of an armaments race, Part I: An anthropological approach. *Bulletin of the Atomic Scientists* 2 (5-6): 10-11.

Bohannan, Paul. 1967. *Law and warfare*. New York: Natural History Press.

Bronowski, J. 1967. *The face of violence*. New York: World Publishing.

Cockran, D. H. 1962. *The Cherokee frontier: Conflict and survival 1740-62*. Norman: University of Oklahoma Press.

Cook, S. F. 1946. Human sacrifices and warfare as factors in the demography of precolonial Mexico. *Human Biology* 18: 82-100.

Coser, Lewis A. 1966. On terminating conflict. In *Readings on modern sociology*. A. Inkeles, ed. Englewood Cliffs, N. J.: Prentice-Hall.

Davie, Maurice. 1929. *The evolution of war*. New Haven: Yale University Press.

Eibel-Eibesfeldt, Irenauss. 1964. Experimental critieria for distinguishing innate from culturally conditioned behavior. In *Cross-cultural understanding: Epistemology in anthropology*. New York: Harper and Row.

Ellis, F. H. 1951. Patterns of aggression and the war cult in Southwestern Pueblos. *Southwestern Journal of Anthropology* 7: 177-201.

Fathauer, George H. 1954. The structure and causation of Mohave warfare. *Southwestern Journal of Anthropology* 10: 97-118.

Freeman, Derek. 1964. Human aggression in anthropological perspective. In *The natural history of aggression*. J. D. Carthy and F. J. Ebling, eds. New York: Academic Press.

Gearing, Fred. 1962. *Priests and warriors: Social structure of Cherokee politics in the 18th Century*. Memoirs of the American Anthropological Association, no. 93.

Grinnell, George B. 1956. *The fighting Cheyennes*. Norman: University of Oklahoma Press.

Hadlock, Wendell. 1947. War among the Northeastern Woodland Indians. *American Anthropologist* 49: 204-221.

Hasluck, M. 1967. The Albanian blood feud. In *Law and warfare*. P. Bohannan, ed. New York: Natural History Press.

Malinowski, B. 1941. War—past, present and future. In *War as a social institution*. J. D. Clarkson and T. C. Cochran, eds. New York: Columbia University Press.

Mead, Margaret. 1940. Warfare is only an invention—not a biological necessity. *Asia* 40:402-405.

————. 1963. The psychology of warless man. In *A warless world*. New York: McGraw-Hill Book Co.

Newcomb, William W., Jr. 1950. A re-examination of the causes of Plains warfare. *American Anthropologist* 52: 317-30.

Secoy, F. R. 1953. *Changing military patterns of the Great Plains*. Monograph of the American Ethnological Society, 21. New York: J.J. Augustin, Pub.

Sission, Roger L., and Russell L. Ackoff. 1967. Toward a theory of the dynamics of conflict. In *Conflict resolution and world education*. S. Mudd, ed. Bloomington, Ind.: Indiana University Press.

Sorokin, P. A. 1942. *Man and society in calamity, the effects of war, revolution, famine, pestilence upon the human mind, behavior, social organization and cultural life*. New York: E. P. Dutton and Co.

Spaulding, Oliver L., H. Nickerson, and J. W. Wright. 1925. *Warfare: A study of military methods from the earliest times*. New York: Harcourt Brace.

Spicer, E. R. 1962. *Cycles of conquest*. Tucson: University of Arizona Press.

Storr, Anthony. 1968. *Human aggression*. New York: Antheneum Press.